OLYMPIC GAMES

Publishers of the International Library

LIBRAIRIE ERNEST FLAMMARION—France
VERLAG J. F. SCHREIBER—Germany
(in association with Union Verlag, Stuttgart, and Oster. Bundesverlag, Vienna)
COLLINS PUBLISHERS—Great Britain
RIZZOLI EDITORE—Italy
FRANKLIN WATTS, INC.—
United States of America

INTERNATIONAL LIBRARY

WOLFGANG GIRARDI

OLYMPIC GAMES

COLLINS · PUBLISHERS
London · Glasgow

FRANKLIN WATTS, INC.
New York

First Edition 1972
Second impression 1974

ISBN: 0 00 100129 9 (*Collins*)
SBN: 531 02105 X (*Franklin Watts*)

Printed and bound in Great Britain by Jarrold & Sons Ltd., Norwich
Library of Congress Catalog Card Number: 72 173604

CONTENTS

CHAPTER 1

THE ANCIENT GAMES

Olympia, site of the ancient Greek Olympic Games, is a pleasantly wooded level valley in the western Peloponnese. It is surrounded by hills on three sides and bounded to the south by the river Alpheus, which flows ten miles eastwards to the Ionian Sea.

On this site, sacred to Zeus and dominated by his great Temple—one of the seven Ancient Wonders of the World—athletes from Greece and the Greek colonies met at four-yearly intervals from 776 BC onwards, for close on 1,200 years, to race, jump and pit their strength against one another in the first organized games meeting ever recorded. Recent excavations have revealed the ground plan of the entire area, known as the Altis or "sacred grove", where on three sides the games took place in front of thousands of spectators. In addition to the great Doric temple of Zeus there was a separate Temple of Hera, lines of colonnades and numerous shrines, altars and statues dotted around the sacred precinct. Beyond the west wall of the Altis were the Gymnasium (with its covered running track), the Palaestra (where the wrestling and boxing took place), the Baths and the Leonidaeum (which housed important guests). Outside the south wall was the Council House and its courtyard with a statue to Zeus where the Olympic oath was taken; and to the east of the Altis was the Stadium where the foot races took place, dating from the 4th century BC and today excavated and restored with its original stone starting and finishing lines.

The Stadium was simply a level rectangular track, about 230 yards long and 35 yards wide, bounded by a low stone parapet with drinking water channels. Up to 10,000 spectators could pack onto the slopes of the hill of Cronus to the north and the artificial embankment on the south, but only the Hellanodicae or judges had proper seats. Three types of foot race were held over this course. One length was the stadion or stade—192·27 metres, or just over 210 yards. The two-length race was the diaulos, and the long-distance contest was the dolichos, the length of which varied but which was up to twenty-four times round the track, or some three miles.

South of the stadium lay the hippodrome for horse and chariot racing. No trace of this has been discovered but it was one of the largest in Greece, with a track at least three-quarters of a mile long.

Origins of the Games

Nobody knows when the Olympic Games began. Official records give the date of the first Olympics as

The Marathon, the race with its beginnings in history

Modern Mexico City: soldiers outside the Aztec Stadium
In the ancient Games no person carrying arms was admitted

776 BC but it is known that a form of religious-cum-musical-cum-athletic festival took place here, as in other places in Greece, centuries earlier. There are two legendary versions of its origins, both related by the poet Pindar. One story claims the festival began in the guise of funeral games at the tomb of Pelops. Pelops, a grandson of Zeus, was a suitor for the hand of Hippodameia, daughter of King Oenomaus of Pisa, near Olympia. With the aid of Poseidon, Pelops defeated and killed Oenomaus in a chariot race (thirteen other suitors having already died in the attempt) and founded a royal dynasty, erecting monuments in the Altis to commemorate the event. The second story attributes the founding of the ancient games to Heracles to celebrate his completion of the fifth labour—cleaning out the stables of Augeas, king of Elis, in a single day. These were evidently located at Olympia and the hero marked out the sacred grove for his father Zeus in thanksgiving, inaugurating the Games, which in-

Opening ceremonies

cluded foot races, wrestling and boxing contests and chariot races.

Be that as it may, the ancient Games date historically from 776 BC with the first foot race winner recorded as Coroebus of Elis. The festival was at first a purely local affair—similar to the Pythian games at Delphi, the Isthmian games at Corinth and the Nemean games between Phlius and Cleonae, though these were of later date. But in time Olympia surpassed its rivals in prestige and scope, attracting competitors and spectators from great distances, to become the most important and spectacular of the Panhellenic national festivals.

Greatest years of the Games

In its heyday—the 5th century

The statue known as the Hercules Farnese in the National Museum, Naples—a copy after the original by the Greek sculptor Lysippos, 4th century BC

Opposite: *The Olympic flame at the 1960 Rome Olympics*

The classical Olympia in Greece

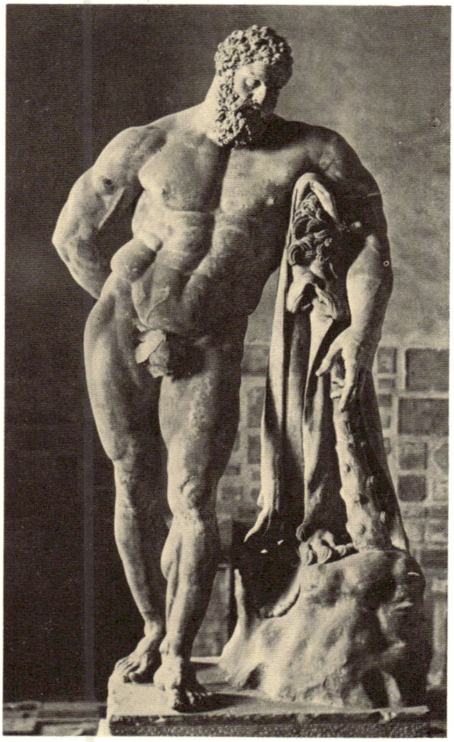

BC—the Games must have been a cross between a pilgrimage and a fair. They took place every four years, usually in late summer, and lasted five days. All disputes and local wars between city states— even foreign wars—were subject to a two-month truce with safe conduct guaranteed to participants and spectators. It was proclaimed by envoys with olive wreaths, and nobody carrying arms was admitted. The first day was set aside for religious observances, including sacrifices, checking in competitors and oath-taking; the next three days were devoted to the athletics proper, and the final day to celebration feasts.

Participation in the athletic events was restricted to men, and later to boys. Women and slaves were not even permitted to watch the games, but women and girls eventually set up a rival meeting, held four-yearly

and confined to foot racing, known as the Heraea. All the Olympic athletes had trained arduously for some ten months prior to the Games but their only reward for winning was a crown of olive leaves, cut from a tree, the sacred olive, with a golden sickle by a Greek boy both of whose parents were living. Nevertheless the winners were otherwise compensated with statues, prizes and honours conferred on them by their home towns when they returned from the Games.

The athletes normally competed unclothed, rubbing their bodies with oil—a practice probably introduced by the Spartans—though races in armour were introduced in 520 BC to complement the existing three sprints and long-distance races. Field events included throwing the diskos or discus, and the javelin. Wrestling and boxing contests formed part of the programme from the start—in the latter the contestants' fists were covered by thin oiled leather thongs, known as the caestus, and later by an open form of boxing glove. In boxing there were no weight categories so the heavyweights had the advantage and fights were of indefinite duration. In 708 BC the pentathlon event was inaugurated—five events demanding all round fitness and prowess—the one-stade foot race, the long jump (apparently a running jump assisted by the swinging of weights), javelin, discus and wrestling. This was the highlight of the Games. Sixty years later the pancration event was introduced—a free-for-all type of boxing and wrestling in which the open fist was used, with hitting and kicking permitted, but eye-gouging forbidden. Chariot racing, both with two and four horses, was held in the hippodrome and other equestrian events were added at various times.

TAPPETO
A

CHAPTER 2

DECLINE AND REVIVAL

It is fitting and quite understandable that the first athletic Games originated in Greece, a nation which set such a price on all-round physical fitness, beauty and strength. Bodily perfection and intellectual achievement were of equal importance, not only for their own sake but also as training for battle—war being an ever-present possibility, whether among rival city states or later, on a national level, against the Persian invader. But the guiding spirit of the Games was friendly and fair competition on a strictly amateur basis and these ideals seem to have been faithfully observed—and rigidly controlled by the judges—during the 6th and 5th centuries BC.

But already a change was evident. Athletes were no longer content merely to take part—their objective was now to win. In this they were encouraged by eager spectators. By the 4th century we see them specializing in a single sport—speed or strength, rarely both—under the watchful guidance of a trainer. A general menu of fruit and milk foods had given way to a special meat-centred diet to enlarge the muscles. The athlete no longer had time for reading, studying, or playing a musical instrument. The body was now built up and the mind neglected—far removed from the earlier ideals. Eminent writers like Socrates and Plato and Euripides complained that athletes did nothing now but eat, drink and sleep.

The arrival of the Romans

The professional athlete had arrived. Possibly standards of performance improved—certainly the same winners' names appear in successive Olympics. But professionalism heralded the gradual decline of the Games. We read of bribery and cheating. When the Romans conquered Greece in the 2nd century BC they kept the Games going in a desultory fashion—unsympathetic to the ancient Greek ideal of sport for its own sake. The number of events dwindled—gladiatorial combat was much more to the Roman taste and the vicious element introduced into boxing was typified by the ugly metal studs, potentially lethal, they added to the older caestus.

Yet the Hellenistic ideals triumphed for a time once Rome had consolidated her imperial power. The festival at Olympia was patronized by emperors, though Nero only won the chariot races and various musical and dramatic events by bribing the judges. Thereafter, degraded and unrecognizable, they plunged rapidly downhill. The 290th Olympics in AD 390 was the last. Four years later the Christian Emperor Theodosius abolished

An ancient sport in an ancient setting at a modern Games. At the Rome Olympics the wrestling events were held in the Roman Forum.

The birthplace of the Olympic Games

them altogether, after 1,166 years.

Destruction and excavation

The sacred site of Olympia had already been desecrated and damaged by barbarian invaders in AD 267. Further conquests and raids denuded it of its treasures, the Temple of Zeus was destroyed by legionaries, and an earthquake in 521 left the Altis bare except for rubble. Finally the river flooded and buried the entire grave under mud and water.

A model of the original Olympia

A French archaeological team in 1829 excavated parts of the great Temple of Zeus and between 1875–1881 German archaeologists cleared the whole Olympic area so that the ancient plan was again revealed, and reconstructions possible. After the Second World War the stadium and other buildings were also excavated. By this time, thanks to the determination and faith of one man, the Olympic Games themselves had been revived.

The vision of Baron de Coubertin

Credit for reviving the modern Olympic Games is commonly given and properly belongs to the French scholar and educationalist, Baron Pierre de Coubertin; but there had in fact been an earlier attempt to reorganize the Games on the ancient Olympic model by a Greek, Major Evangelios Zappas, in 1859. For lack of a proper stadium and official backing Zappas staged his Games in the streets of Athens itself. It was a chaotic affair with many injuries among the spectators, nor was a second meeting, in 1870 after Zappas' death, any more encouraging, two of the potential entrant nations being otherwise engaged in a conflict far removed from the Olympic spirit. It was left to Coubertin, deeply read in the Greek classics and a profound admirer of the ancient Greek sporting ideals, to call a meeting of sportsmen in Paris in 1892 (which aroused little enthusiasm), and then to persist by convening an international Olympic Congress in the Sorbonne in July 1894, where the response proved encouraging beyond his wildest dreams.

Coubertin was no sportsman himself, but as an educationalist envisaged physical activity as an

Obverse and reverse of a gold medal from the Mexico City Games. Gold medals were first introduced at the 1908 Olympics

essential feature of an all-round education. He had been much impressed by a visit to Dr Arnold's public school at Rugby and felt that such a curriculum, with its emphasis on athletics, could profitably be copied by French institutions of education. But his humanitarian interests drew him towards wider horizons until he became obsessed with the idea of reviving the ancient Olympic Games, in which the original noble ideals of amateur sport, practised for its own sake, could find modern expression. He envisaged regular international sports gatherings in which athletes would compete on a friendly footing, oblivious of national loyalties and rivalries, a creed which he outlined at the Paris meeting of 1892 and expanded in a letter sent out to all delegations to the 1894 Congress. His proposal to revive the Olympic Games received warm support from all the participating nations, notably Great Britain, the United States, France, Italy, Spain, Sweden, Russia, Belgium and Greece, while messages of support came from other countries such as Hungary, Holland and Australia.

The Olympic torch burns once again

Appropriately, it was agreed the venue for the 1st Olympics would be Athens two years later. Fortunately, though only after long persuasion, money was forthcoming from the Greek government out of funds left by Major Zappas and his brother, and a subscription list was headed by the wealthy George Averoff, who contributed a million drachma to build a marble Olympic Stadium, with a capacity of 60,000 spectators. Finally, on a bleak and wet spring morning in 1896, to the accompaniment of bands and the release of flocks of doves, the lighting of the torch carried by relay from Olympia took place.

One athlete on behalf of all the others took the Olympic oath: "In the name of all competitors I promise that we will take part in these Olympic Games, respecting and abiding by the rules which govern them, in the true spirit of sportsmanship, for the glory of sport and for the honour of our teams." Then the King of Greece declared the Games open.

A fighting helmet, worn in the classical Olympic Games, in the Olympia Museum

Above right: *The punchbag was used in boxing training over two thousand years ago*

The spirits of the ardently patriotic Greek spectators were dashed from the start as the American athletes proceeded to sweep all the field events (the favoured Greek discus thrower Paraskevopoulos was surprisingly beaten by 8 inches) while Thomas Burke of the United States and Edwin Flack of Australia shared the sprints and the long-distance races. But the Greeks had their moment of glory in the Marathon.

Pheidippides and Spiridon Louis

This long-distance running event

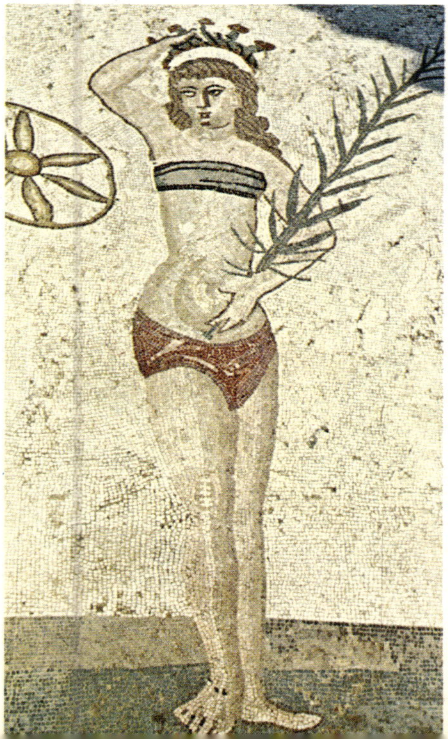

In ancient times women were not allowed to take part in the Olympic Games. But they did practise sport, for which they wore a kind of bikini. Roman mosaic from the 14th century AD in the Piazza Armerina, Sicily

was not part of the programme of the ancient Games and the idea of including it, to commemorate the historic victory of the Greeks over the Persians at Marathon in 490 BC, belonged to another Frenchman, Michel Bréal. According to legend—or history—a Greek messenger named Pheidippides carried the news of the victory on foot to the citizens of Athens and fell dead on his arrival. Bréal suggested that the race to be known as the Marathon be run over approximately the same course from the ridge of the modern town of Marathon to the stadium at Athens, a distance of almost 40 kilometres. There were 25 starters, most of them Greek, who were accompanied over the dusty roads and mountain trails by Greek cavalry. Many of them went off at the starter's gun as if they were competing in a sprint and were soon overcome by the dust and the afternoon heat. Favourites included the Australian Flack (winner of the 800 and 1,500 metres), Arthur Blake of the USA, Albin Lemursiaux of France, and it was Lemursiaux who set the cracking pace for 30 kilometres until he was overtaken on an uphill stretch by Flack. The race seemed won, and word to that effect was buzzing round the depressed stadium when, about 5 kilometres from the finish, Flack was in turn passed by an unknown

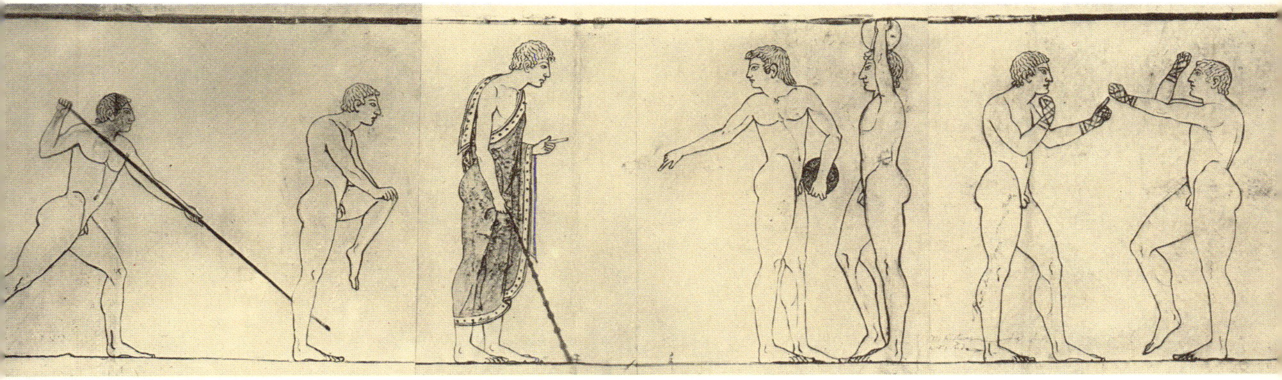

Greek shepherd named Spiridon Louis—a competitor given no chance of success. Horsemen brought the incredible news that Greeks were now occupying the first three places. Then, amid scenes of near pandemonium, the diminutive figure of Louis trundled into the stadium. Two Greek princes, George and Constantine, each 6½ feet tall, leapt onto the track to flank the little man as he chugged up to the finishing line and up to the Royal Box. The crowd went wild, their delight completed by the arrival—a full seven minutes later—of Louis' compatriot Haralambos Vasilakos. The third Greek runner, Velokas, was disqualified for having accepted a lift on the way, third place going to the Hungarian Kellner.

Curiously Greece also triumphed in the long-distance cycle race from Marathon to Athens and back, their only win ever in this sport, the French sweeping the other events. As a fitting climax and conclusion to Baron de Coubertin's Ist Olympics all competitors and officials who had participated in the Games were entertained to a royal breakfast by the King of Greece. The modern Games had truly begun.

In an Etruscan grave at Tarquinia, wall paintings dating from the 5th century AD have been discovered showing athletes at an ancient sports ground. They include a pole-vaulter, an athlete massaging his leg, a judge holding a crook, discus throwers and boxers

Fighting scenes. Wall painting in an Etruscan grave at Chiusi

CHAPTER 3

THE MODERN OLYMPICS—FROM PARIS TO MELBOURNE

In tribute to Baron de Coubertin the IInd Games were held in Paris. But the splendid organization and high excitement of the Athens Olympiad had disappeared four years later. Although there were 13 competing nations few bothered to send fully representative teams—almost all the 55 American athletes came from the New York Athletic Club or from college teams—and the Games, staged on a makeshift grass course in the grounds of the Racing Club de France, received no publicity. In fact they were regarded as nothing more than a sideshow of the 1900 Paris Exhibition. The general confusion and muddle was typified by the arrangements made for opening the Games, on Saturday July 14—Bastille Day, when Parisians would doubtless have other ways of celebrating. A proposal to put the opening forward to the Sunday drew scandalized protests from the Sabbath observers, including most of the Americans. In fact the games opened on the Saturday before a very sparse and uninterested crowd and many of the leading athletes refused to take part in the heats and finals on the Sunday.

The Americans dominate track and field

Yet, in spite of these half-hearted preparations and the public apathy, there were some creditable performances, most of them by the Americans who once again dominated the track and field events, winning 17 out of 23. (Incidentally no official tally is kept of team scores in Olympics but it has never been possible to eliminate national rivalry—even if it is unofficial!) The great all-rounder Alvin Kraenzlein, pioneer of modern hurdling, won both the low and high hurdles as well as the 60 metres dash and the long jump. Kraenzlein's time for the 200 metres hurdles was 25·4 seconds, though he had previously set up a world record in 1898 of 23·6 seconds, equalled but not surpassed for 25 years. In the long jump Kraenzlein's closest rival was his American colleague Myer Prinstein, then the world record holder. Both men, using the new fast run-up technique, had jumped over 24 feet, and when Prinstein withdrew because of the Sunday competition Kraenzlein went on to win easily with a relatively short jump of 23 feet $6\frac{7}{8}$ inches.

Another remarkable American athlete, Ray Ewry, who had been paralysed in the legs as a child and had taken to athletics for health reasons, chalked up three successes in the standing high jump, standing long jump and standing hop, step and jump (triple jump). Ewry was

Ancient Olympia today: the remains of Palaestra

Plato approved of the Olympics. Bust in the Vatican Museum, Rome

Baron Pierre de Coubertin—founder of the modern Olympic Games

Avery Brundage, the President of the International Olympic Committee (second from left) *inspects a model of the site for the Munich Games*

to repeat this triple success in the 1904 Games and to win two more gold medals in 1908. All these standing jump events were discontinued after the First World War.

Britain, also not taking the Games very seriously, took four of the track events, including the relay, and their swimming star, J. Jarvis, won three freestyle races.

The Marathon, which had provided such drama at Athens, also was disappointing, though once again it provided a local winner in the person of a Paris baker's assistant named Michel Théato, who showed the necessary stamina in enduring a complicated course through the Paris streets in a temperature of 102°F!

St Louis Olympics—1904

The lack of enthusiasm and disorganization of the Paris Games were virtually duplicated in the IIIrd

Photographs taken at the first modern Olympic Games at Athens in 1896.
Above: *The start of the 100 metres* Below: *The pole-vault*

USA
311

Olympics in St Louis in 1904. The venue was particularly ill-advised despite America's legitimate claim, in view of her 1900 successes, to hold the Games on her home ground. Regarded again as a secondary attraction compared with the St Louis World Fair, the distance and the travelling expense involved proved too much for most nations and only about eight bothered to attend from abroad, with Great Britain and France boycotting them entirely. Not unnaturally, therefore, the United States athletes once more had things all their own way, turning in some remarkably fine performances in the process. They won 21 of the 22 track and field events, the Canadian Etienne Desmarteau taking the special 56-lb shot putt to prevent an absolutely clean sweep.

Two veterans of the Paris Games, Ewry and Prinstein shared most of the jumping prizes, the latter winning the running long jump and triple jump on the same day. Archie Hahn, the Michigan sprinter, won the 60, 100 and 200 metres, and his team-mate Harry Hillman the 400 metres and 200 and 400 metres hurdles. In the longer distance events James Lightbody set new world records in winning the 800 metres in 1:56 and the 1,500 in 4:05·4. He went on to win the 2,500 metres steeplechase into the bargain.

In the throwing events the genial Irish-American policeman, Martin Sheridan, won the discus, as he was to do four years later, confirming him as the unofficial world record holder, an honour held in the shot putt by his compatriot Ralph Rose. Rose won the event with a mighty throw of 48 feet 7 inches, and later achieved 51 feet $\frac{3}{4}$ inch for the official world record, held for 15 years. Completing the American trio was another Irish-American, John Flanagan, who won the hammer throw—as he had done at Paris and was to do again in London—a record three in a row.

In the "fringe" events Cuba swept the board in the fencing and a great new American swimmer, Charles Daniels, emerged to take two firsts, a second and a third place in the freestyle races.

A comical Marathon

Once again the Marathon provided all the drama—and a good deal of amusement. The field included 17 Americans, 10 Greeks, two black South Africans and Felix Carvajal of Cuba. A postman by profession, Carvajal had set up a soapbox in the streets of Havana and persuaded passers-by to subscribe towards his fare. He arrived at the start wearing walking shoes, a long-sleeved shirt and long trousers, which he permitted a bystander to trim into shorts with some shears. But nobody came forward with any running shoes! He more than held his own in the appallingly hot and dusty conditions—a cavalcade of motor cars following the race hardly made conditions better—chatted genially to the spectators, at one stage snatched some peaches from the driver of a car and trotted into the stadium in fourth place. Other competitors failed to complete the gruelling course, one of them collapsing and almost dying of a stomach haemorrhage. Another, who did finish, was chased for several miles by a fierce dog. The official winner was Thomas Hicks, who had been among the leaders all the way but who was in such a bad state in the final stages that he had to be kept going with minute doses of strychnine and more copious supplies of eggs and brandy. But Hicks was not the first across

Strength and determination personified. Bill Toomey, winner of the decathlon at the 1968 Olympics

No loneliness for this long-distance runner during the Marathon at the Tokyo Olympics

the finishing line—that moment of glory went to the American Fred Lorz, a full $2\frac{1}{2}$ hours previously. He was about to receive the winner's wreath from President Theodore Roosevelt's daughter Alice when somebody accused him of cheating. Sure enough, evidence was produced to show that Lorz had secured a lift from a passing car when attacked by stomach cramps after some nine miles. The car had broken down and dropped Lorz about five miles from the stadium and he had decided to run the rest of the way. Probably there had been no intention to cheat—merely to play a practical joke on his opponents, the crowd and the Olympic authorities. The last named were especially unamused and banned Lorz from athletics for life.

Refreshments for the Marathon runners in Tokyo

The 1906 Athenian Celebration

The 1906 Athenian Celebration, as it was called, is not ranked as an official Olympics, and most of the record books do not trouble to list the winners. It had been planned at the end of the Ist Olympics as an alternative to the Olympic Games, to take place in Athens every four years between the Olympics proper. This in fact was the only one to be held, but although unofficial it proved enormously popular, with 19 nations entering 900 athletes. Many of the victors of the 1904 and subsequent 1908 Olympics repeated their successes in the great marble stadium, but unexpected victories in the 400 and 800 metres were recorded by an unofficial young American competitor, Paul Pilgrim. The javelin event was held for the first time (an event with which the Americans were unfamiliar) and was won by the experienced Swedish record holder Erik Lemming, who proved his supremacy by winning the gold medals in the following two official Olympics. Association football was part of the programme for the first time, with Denmark beating Smyrna in the final. And the honour of the Marathon was restored—without any cheating or other mishaps—though this time the Greek runners were eclipsed, the winner being Billy Sherring of Canada, in a close finish in a new record time of 2 hours 51 minutes 18·4 seconds, over 7 minutes better than Spiridon Louis in 1896.

The first London Games —1908

On July 13 1908, King Edward VII opened the IVth Olympics before a capacity crowd of 70,000 in the new White City stadium at Shepherd's Bush, London. The Games were attended by competitors from 19 nations and although they got off to a somewhat shaky start—Finland complaining that they were not allowed to carry their national flag in the opening parade, and Sweden and the USA pointing out that their flags were not flying above the stadium—the Games were keenly competed and well attended. Exception was also taken—justifiably—to the fact that all the judges were British, and there were allegations of their partiality. Certainly one incident in which they were involved resulted in much bitter feeling. This was the final of the 400 metres, in which the British runner Wyndham Halswelle was declared to have been impeded and crowded off the track by one, possibly two Americans. The officials ordered the race to be rerun on another day and Halswelle was left to jog around the track unopposed for an empty victory. His prize incidentally, as for all the winners, was a gold medal, the first time these had been awarded at a Games.

There was more drama and controversy over the Marathon, which was run from the lawn at Windsor Castle to the White City Stadium, a distance of 26 miles 385 yards. Strangely, this quite arbitrary distance was henceforth fixed as the official distance for the race. The Americans had already protested that the North American Indian, Tom Longboat, running for Canada, should be banned from the race because he was a professional, but to no avail. On a hot afternoon —the weather had been variable until then—56 runners started off towards London. The pace took its customary toll, and with only a couple of miles to go, the leader was South Africa's Charles Hefferon.

The American Indian Jim Thorpe from Oklahoma, to whom the King of Sweden said, "Sir, you are the greatest athlete in the world!"

Then on the last stretch he was overtaken by the small Italian runner Dorando Pietri. The Italian's superhuman effort, however, almost killed him. Dazed and gasping for breath, he entered the huge stadium, then turned right instead of left and collapsed a short way down the track. As officials rushed towards him the crowd yelled advice, some urging that the prostrate runner be helped up, others (mindful of the rules) that he be left to recover under his own steam. Yielding to human instincts, doctors and officials helped him to his feet and steered him in the right direction. The gallant Italian stumbled again and fell and was once more pulled to his feet, and practically carried over the finishing line. Almost at once he was borne off on a stretcher. Meanwhile the American John Hayes had overtaken Hefferon and had finished only half a minute behind Pietri. A protest was lodged and Hayes declared the winner. But in the minds of the spectators the Italian had won, and to the satisfaction of all concerned he was presented with a replica of the gold cup awarded to Hayes.

In less controversial events, Sweden's Erik Lemming won two javelin contests, the American Mel Sheppard turned in record times in winning the 800 and 1,500 metres, and Britain's G. E. Larner took first place in both of the newly introduced walking events. The great American athlete Martin Sheridan—also a shot putter—won the discus as in the 1904 and unofficial 1906 Olympics. Archery and skating were among other events forming part of the Olympic programme for the first time.

Baron de Coubertin was not happy about the London Games. They had been too expensive (deficit of about £19,000), had attempted too much (with insufficient emphasis on athletics), and they had been marred by international squabbles. The organizers of the 1912 games held in Sweden learned from these mistakes and succeeded in staging the most successful Games to date.

Jim Thorpe—hero and "villain" of Stockholm

An American Indian athlete was again the centre of controversy in the Vth Olympics in Stockholm. His name was Jim Thorpe, and though he easily won the new all-round events of the pentathlon and decathlon he was later stripped of his medals and disqualified for "professionalism". Somebody had discovered that he had once played a baseball game for money!

Thorpe, an enormously powerful man, was a footballer who came comparatively late to athletics and had an instinctive dislike for systematic training. This did not prevent him winning first the pentathlon (long jump, javelin, 200 metres, discus and 1,500 metres) and then

Paavo Nurmi ran against the clock, literally—with a stop-watch in his hand

the decathlon—ten events spread over three days. It was undoubtedly the greatest all-round achievement in the annals of sport. The taxing decathlon called for above average ability in the 100, 400 and 1,500 metres runs, 110 metres hurdles, the long and high jumps, the pole vault, the shot putt, discus and javelin. Thorpe finished first in the running and hurdle events, the high jump and the pole vault, the discus and shot putt, hundreds of points ahead of the second-placed Swede, Hugo Wieslander. But his glory was short lived. The following year he was instructed to return his cups and medals and his name was struck off the list of winners. Nevertheless King Gustav V had proclaimed him to be the greatest athlete in the world and decades later—after his death in 1953—a town was named in his honour with the King's tribute inscribed on his memorial. Incidentally, one of the other competitors in the Stockholm Games was a young American named Avery Brundage.

In every other respect the Stockholm Games were a triumph, the first to come anywhere near to fulfilling the noble ideals envisaged by de Coubertin. The splendid stadium, which was converted overnight into a show ring for the equestrian events, was smaller than previous ones, accommodating just over 20,000 people; but a record number of 3,282 competitors from 27 nations took part. The organization was streamlined, the judging made easier by the introduction of electrical timing and photo-finish devices, and spectators' interest—particularly in the field events—sustained by running commentaries over the new public address system. There were more than 100 different events in the programme including swimming and diving for women in the fine Olympic-sized pool. There was also a series of artistic competitions in which it is interesting to note the name of Baron de Coubertin appeared as prize winner for literature.

Runners at the finishing tape, in varying postures of exhaustion

Many track and field records were shattered at Stockholm, one of the many exciting moments coming in the final of the 800 metres when America's nineteen-year-old Ted Meredith broke the tape a tenth of a second ahead of the favourite Mel Sheppard and a third American, Ira Davenport. Indeed five runners appeared to have finished in an unprecedented dead heat, but the camera sorted them out with a mere two-fifths of a second separating first from fifth place. Meredith and Sheppard also led the Americans to a comfortable victory in the 1600 metres relay—the first time it had been included.

First of the "Flying Finns"

The Americans dominated the sprints but were outclassed in the longer distances. Britain's Arnold Jackson came up in the last 30 metres and held them all off to win the 1,500 metres in a record Olympic time of 3:56·8 in yet another photo-finish, with less than a second separating him from the fifth com-

Sonja Henie, the "princess of the ice", at the height of her career, and some years later standing with her husband Nils Onstad in front of a painting by Fernand Leger—part of her valuable art collection

petitor. But the hero of the Games was the first in a great line of "Flying Finns", Hannes Kolehmainen, who raced off with the gold medals in three new events—the 5,000 metres, the 10,000 metres and (the only time it was held) the 8,000 metres cross-country race. This phenomenal runner, a cheerful and popular figure of slender physique, started by winning his heat of the 10,000 metres (in later Games this was dispensed with) and then, the very next day, the final in 31:20·8. The next day, still fresh and smiling, the amazing Finn won his heat of the 5,000 metres in a world record time of 15:05·0. In his fourth distance race in four days—the final of the 5,000 metres—he fought a tremendous duel with the idolized French champion, Jean Bouin, edging him out by a mere second at the tape in an astounding world record time of 14:36·6. After one day's rest Kolehmainen proceeded to set up another world mark in a heat of the 3,000 metres team race (his colleagues failing however to boost him to the final), and three days later romped home for a third gold medal in the cross-country race. Finland's run of successes were continued by Armas Taipole who won the two discus events, and Juho Saaristo who took Finland's sixth gold medal for the "two-handed" javelin throw.

The Marathon also provided its usual thrills. The course began and ended in the stadium and traffic was banned. Kolehmainen's elder brother was among the runners, but first and second place were taken by the South Africans Kenneth McArthur and Chris Gitsham.

The highly successful games ended amid cheerful promises to meet at the VIth Olympics in Berlin four years later. The fateful events of August 1914 put an end to those hopes and marked the end of the first phase of the modern Olympic Games.

The VIIth Olympics—Antwerp 1920

The honour of holding the first post-war Games went to Belgium in place of Hungary who, as a defeated nation, was not invited. Barely recovered from the scars of the four-year conflict, the Belgians put on a brave show and the opening ceremony with the parade of nations led by Greece was a particularly moving occasion, as the athletes lined up in the stadium to take the Olympic oath with the five-circled Olympic flag inscribed with de Coubertin's chosen motto—"Citius, Altius, Fortius" (swifter, higher, stronger)—flying for the first time.

Despite the unrepresentative nature of the Games, and the tragic gaps in the ranks of athletes whose careers had promised so much eight years previously, the Games included many dramatic highlights in which the hard-training and dedicated Finns featured prominently. In the very first event, the javelin throw, they took all three medals, then achieved a gold and silver in both the shot putt and the discus. The great American sprinter, Charley Paddock, then on the verge of a record-breaking career lasting a decade, won the 100 metres, thanks to a flying start, in 10·8 seconds and finished second in the 200 metres. South Africa's Bevil Rudd took the 400 metres and Britain's Albert Hill won both the 800 and 1,500 metres. But, as so many times before, the real excitement was reserved for the long-distance events. Winner of the 5,000 metres was a small 21-year-old Frenchman named Joseph Guillemot, a full 4·4 seconds ahead of a stocky, serious-faced Finn, two years older than he, whose name was soon to make athletics history—Paavo Nurmi.

The incomparable Nurmi

Nurmi was temperamentally the opposite of his boyhood hero Hannes Kolehmainen. Forced to help support his family as an errand boy after the early death of his father, poverty and wartime deprivation had shaped his character and outlook. He was not one to win the spectators' hearts with a lackadaisical manner and a sunny smile. Dour, unsmiling and utterly dedicated to his chosen career, Nurmi was as yet hardly known outside Finland. And on his first appearance in the Olympics, though he impressed by leading the field almost all the way, the fact that he had been overtaken and fairly beaten by the Frenchman gave no hint at all of the amazing powers soon to be revealed to the world. It was three days after his disappointing debut that his legendary career really began. Once again he battled it out over the

Plaster figures at the Olympic Games

Birger Rouud, winner of the ski-jumping gold in 1932 and 1936

uneven course with the Frenchman. But this time he judged his race better and with a tremendous burst of speed left Guillemot standing on the final stretch, to win his first gold medal by eight metres. Three days later he proved that the victory in the 10,000 metres was no accident as he coasted home in the final 200 metres of the 9,000 metre cross-country race. The following year was to see Nurmi set up a world record in the 10,000 metres (30:40·2, well over a minute better than his Olympic time), the first of 20 distance records to stand to his credit during his amazing eleven-year career.

It was however, the "veteran" Kolehmainen, now resident in the United States, who provided a worthy climax to the Games by entering the Marathon with 34 other competitors. On a cool, showery afternoon, the 1912 triple gold medalist bided his time until about halfway when he moved up with the leaders, the South African 1912 Marathon silver medalist, Gitsham and the Estonian, Jüri Lossman. The South African dropped out with a leg injury a couple of miles from the finish, at which point Kolehmainen raced past Lossman. The younger man, however, held on gamely and the Finn had to summon up every ounce of his waning strength to win, in the closest finish ever, by 12·8 seconds. The time proved faster than McArthur's at Stockholm and the course, when measured, proved to be 26 miles 990 yards—the longest Marathon ever run. The exultant Finnish spectators wrapped their hero in a Finnish flag and bore him triumphantly in a well-deserved lap of honour.

Ski-jumpers airborne at the Innsbruck Olympics, 1964

The Italians made their mark at the VIIth Olympics, with five out of a possible six golds in fencing, one each for the gymnastic individual and team events, and two for walking, both events being won by Ugo Frigerio.

Nurmi's finest hour—Paris 1924

In 1924 Paris held the Olympics for the second time, this time a splendidly organized affair at Colombes Stadium. But before the VIIIth Olympics opened in July—and in response to growing demands of skiing enthusiasts throughout Europe—the French Olympic Committee held a winter sports festival in the Alpine resort of Chamonix in January. Eighteen nations took part and the popular success of the meeting led the International Olympic Committee to give its sanction to a four-yearly sports festival during the winter preceding the Olympics themselves.

The first Winter Olympics at Chamonix set the pattern for subsequent competitions, featuring figure and speed skating, ski racing and jumping, four man bobsled and ice hockey. Austria, Finland and Norway shared most of the skating and skiing medals, with Switzerland taking the bobsled event and Canada the ice hockey. In the ladies figure skating the competitors included a little eleven-year-old Norwegian girl, who was placed last. Her name was Sonja Henie, and the following year she became Norwegian champion. Most successful individual contestants were Finland's Clas Thunberg with three medals (two gold and a silver) for speed skating and Norway's Thorleif Haug who won all three distance skiing events.

Two golds in an hour

In the Summer Olympics Finland

215
1964
INNSBRUCK
245
1964
INNSBRUCK
33
1964
INNSBRUCK
376
1964
INNSBRUCK
251

The magnificent Owens at the 1936 Olympic Games in Berlin

once more gave notice of her intentions to equal if not better her performance in the 1920 Games. Nurmi's arch-rival Ville Ritola clipped 12 seconds off the world record in the 10,000 metres, while his compatriot Jonni Myrrä, winner at Antwerp, repeated his triumph in the javelin throw. Ritola then proceeded to win the 3,000 metres steeplechase, also in a record time. Meanwhile the packed stadium waited breathlessly for the clash between the two great Finnish distance runners in the 5,000 metres. Nurmi was now at the peak of his form, carrying out a rigorous daily schedule, stop-watch in hand, and currently the holder of both the 1,500 and 5,000 metres world records. Kohlemainen had won both races in 1912; Nurmi was determined to repeat the feat. He won his heat of the 5,000 on July 8 and of the 1,500 the following day. This left him with both finals to run on the afternoon of July 10—and within 55 minutes of each other! He had no trouble with the 1,500 metres, pounding round the 500 metre course with his familiar powerful stride, head up, chest out, periodically glancing at his stop-watch and tossing it aside as his searing pace left the rest of the field far behind, a second outside his own world record in 3:53·6. He then retired to the dressing room for a rest and within the hour was back among the starters for the epic 5,000 metres final.

Ville Ritola, the 10,000 metres winner and world record holder, was just as grimly determined as Nurmi to prove that he was Finland's and the world's number

At the 1960 Olympics in Rome the long run of victories by black sprinters was broken by a European: Armin Hary of West Germany

one distance runner. And Edvin Wide—also born in Finland but competing for Sweden—was equally intent on beating them both. Nurmi had already beaten Wide in a challenge mile in Stockholm the previous year in a world record time, and the Swede was eager for revenge. Trusty stop-watch in hand, Paavo Nurmi, impassive as ever, allowed both Ritola and Wide to set a cracking pace over the first 1,000 metres, then overtook them both at the halfway mark. With the spectators roaring him on he redoubled his efforts, leaving Wide hopelessly out of touch. Ritola, however, hung on grimly and on the home stretch was only a few strides behind. Nurmi kept up his elegant rhythm, and, full of confidence, put on a final spurt to take the gold medal by one-fifth of a second. It was a sweet victory and he repeated it two days later when, in a temperature of 102°F, he beat Ritola again in the gruelling 9,000 metres cross-country run through the streets of Paris—this time by well over a minute. In such form Nurmi, had he so elected, could probably have won the Marathon too, but he did not compete and the race—comparatively uneventful for a change—was won by yet another Finnish runner, Albin Stenroos.

The Flying Finn was undoubtedly the hero of the VIIIth Olympics but there were other fine performances, especially by British athletes. In the 100 metres sprint Harold Abrahams turned in a wonderfully consistent performance, beating favoured American runners such as Charley Paddock, Jackson Scholz and Loren Murchison, winning two heats and the final in the same time, 10·6 seconds. Scholz came back to win the 200 metres, but the Scottish divinity student Eric Liddell upset the pundits in the 400 metres. Though no stylist, with his head flung back and arms flailing, Liddell thundered round the outside lane of the Colombes track at a searing pace. At the halfway mark he was clocked at 22·2 and he held off the field to win in an Olympic record time of 47·6 seconds. And Britain made it a trio of gold medals when Douglas Lowe narrowly defeated the Swiss Paul Martin in the 800 metres.

The Americans, as expected, dominated the hurdles, the relays, the jumps and the throwing events. Harold Osborn cleared 6 feet 6 inches to win the high jumps and went on to win the decathlon—an achievement never equalled—and Clarence (Bud) Houser also took two golds, for the discus and shot putt. Meanwhile in the swimming pool a muscular young American named Johnny Weissmuller won the 100 metres and 400 metres freestyles, a prelude to a distinguished career which was to earn him world fame as the best known of cinema's Tarzans.

The IXth Games—Amsterdam 1928

1928 saw the second winter sports Games held at St Moritz in Switzerland, and a fuller programme than four years previously. Delighting the spectators and now approaching the peak of her form, the 15-year-old Norwegian champion Sonja Henie took the women's figure skating crown, a feat she repeated in the 1932 and 1936 games. In addition to her three Olympic gold medals the popular little blonde skater was to win ten world championships and go on to a spectacularly successful film career. Meanwhile Sweden's ace male figure skater, Gillis Grafström was collecting his third successive

For a photographer, the Olympic Games are often as strenuous as they are for the athletes!

Fanny Blankers-Koen competing in the 80 metres hurdles in the 1948 London Games

gold medal, while Finland's Clas Thunberg took two more speed skating titles. Norway again won the ski jumping and Canada successfully defended her ice hockey crown.

For the IXth Olympics in Amsterdam, the Dutch built a stadium seating 40,000 people on reclaimed swamp-land and entertained over 4,000 athletes from 43 nations. It rained for much of the time but the Dutch, experienced in such matters, ensured that the course was well drained and conditions were tolerable. The Games were notable for the introduction of track and field events for women, for the continuance of Finland's supremacy in the distance running, for the new challenges which came from the previously excluded German runners and for the first gold medal ever for a Japanese athlete. From the American viewpoint too the Games were memorable, in a less happy manner. Not only did they lose three events in which they had previously been unbeaten—the low and high hurdles and the hammer throw—but they only managed to capture one gold medal for individual running (the relays as usual went to them), a football player named Ray Barbuti winning a photo-finish in the 400 metres.

The first and most complete surprises came in the 100 and 200 metre sprints in which the great Californian Frank Wykoff and other American stars were soundly beaten by an unknown Canadian schoolboy, Percy Williams. The astonishing 19-year-old, who had hitch-hiked across Canada in order to compete, won the 100 metres in 10·8 seconds, then whipped the 200 metres field, including the experienced German Helmut Körnig and the British Walter Rangeley, in 21·8 seconds. Douglas Lowe defended his 800 metres title and scored another unexpected but deserved triumph over the favourite, the American Lloyd Hahn. And there were further shocks for the Americans as Britain's David Cecil, otherwise known as Lord Burghley, romped off with the 400 metres hurdles, and South Africa's Sid Atkinson came first in the 110 metres hurdles. Then, in the longer distances, Finland's versatile runners continued to show other competitors their heels. Nor was it simply a two-man show by the great pair Ritola and Nurmi, by now both past their absolute peak though still capable of record times. The 1,500 metres, for example, went to Harri Larva, a young watchmaker, who beat the magnificent little French runner Jules Ladoumègue by three-fifths of a second. Then in the 5,000 metres Ritola and Nurmi fought out their 1924 battle again. This time Ritola had his revenge with a two-second victory in a comparatively slow time. Nurmi also had to be content with a silver medal in the 3,000 metres steeplechase, behind his team-mate Toivo Loukola. To the crowd's consternation, he had actually fallen in his heat and been courteously helped to his feet by the Frenchman, Lucien Duquesne. This was the Olympic crowd's last glimpse of the fabulous Nurmi, a legend of the track.

There were some surprises in the field events too, notably in the hammer throw, when the massive Irishman, Dr Pat O'Callaghan, a pupil of the great John Flanagan, took the gold medal. America, however, redeemed herself with splendid victories in the high jump, long jump, pole vault and shot putt. Bud Houser retained his discus crown and the javelin throw went to Sweden's record-breaker Erik Lundkvist. The triple jump saw victory go to Mikio Oda, who had finished sixth at Paris—this being the first gold medal ever for Japan. Finally Finland's Paavo Yrjola took the gold for the decathlon with a new points record.

New attractions at the Games

The women's events—five track and field as well as gymnastics, fencing, swimming and diving—provided added interest for spectators. Canada's Ethel Catherwood was popularly acclaimed both for her good looks and her high jumping; German women won the 800 metres and the foils; and in the discus Poland's Halinaa Konopacka became the first of a succession of East European champions in women's field events.

There remained only the Marathon on the final day and it proved to be a fiercely contested race with the lead changing continually. The strong team of Finnish runners was always a threat and two Japanese runners also did well. But the winner was a thickset Algerian mechanic named El Ouafi (running of course for France), who won by 26 seconds from a Chilean newsboy named Miguel Plaza.

Dick Button of the USA performing one of his stupendous jumps. He won two successive golds at figure skating

Thanks to the mass-media, people all over the world can now see and read about the Olympics. Left: *A television camera in Innsbruck.* Right: *An excited press gallery in Cortina*

Los Angeles Olympics 1932

Hosts for the Xth Olympic Games were the United States; the near perfect setting chosen was Los Angeles on the west coast. As a prelude to the Games proper the IIIrd Winter Games were staged at Lake Placid, 2,000 feet up in New York's Adirondack Mountains. American skaters, performing on home ice, made almost a clean sweep of the speed events, while the incomparable Sonja Henie and Austria's Karl Schafer took the individual figure skating crowns. Snow conditions for the skiing events proved surprisingly good and honours were shared by Sweden, Norway and Finland, with Norway's Birger Rouud winning the ski jumping. Canada beat America in the ice hockey final, but both bobsled events were won by the host country. With over 350 competitors from 17 nations competing and enthusiastic crowds for both indoor and outdoor events, official confidence in the future of the Winter Games had been fully justified.

The worldwide economic depression was perhaps the only cloud hanging over the Summer Games, which opened on July 30 in the immense new stadium at Los Angeles with its capacity seating for 105,000 spectators. The superb track and field conditions encouraged the 2,000 athletes from 39 nations to turn in magnificent performances and though there was no obvious hero of the games, the crowds were treated to a feast of record breaking. Furthermore, the organization was streamlined, the male competitors being housed for the first time in their own Olympic Village on a 250-acre site outside the city.

Herb Elliott, inspired by Kuts at Melbourne, an inspiration himself at Rome

Mixed fortunes for the Finns

There was keen disappointment, however, at the official decision not to allow the great Nurmi to compete, on the grounds that he had waived his amateur status by accepting payment for races recently run in Germany. Yet tiny Finland still managed to produce two long-distance gold medallists in Lauri Lehtinen, who won a thrilling 5,000 metres final in a photo-finish from the American Ralph Hill, and Volmari Iso-Hollo in the 3,000 metres steeplechase. It was only discovered after scrutinizing the times of the latter race that the runners had in fact covered one lap too many—but by mutual agreement the result was allowed to stand!

The Finns, however, had a shock in two other races in which they held very high hopes. In the 10,000 metres final, with Iso-Hollo and second-string Lauri Virtanen hoping to take the first two places, a virtually unknown Pole named Janusz Kusocinski held them both off to win in an Olympic record time of 30:11·4. Later, in the star-studded final of the 1,500 metres, Finland's three contestants included the 1928 gold medallist Harri Larva, while others hotly tipped included Britain's Jerry

Cornes, New Zealand's Jack Lovelock, Canada's Phil Edwards and America's Glenn Cunningham. Cunningham and Edwards led until the last lap but Lovelock and Cornes were gaining on them with every stride. So too was Italy's stocky Luigi Beccali, noted for his sprint finish, but not seriously considered against this competition. Beccali, however, astonished the entire stadium by sprinting past the tiring Cunningham and Edwards on the home stretch and breaking the tape some five yards ahead of Cornes in a new Olympic record.

Local boys come good

In most of the other track and field events traditionally won by American athletes, the local boys did not disappoint. The two great black sprinters Eddie Tolan and Ralph Metcalfe clashed in the 100 and 200 metres finals, with Tolan winning both in record-shattering times of 10·3 seconds and 21·2 seconds respectively. The 400 metres was a dramatic all-American affair bringing together Bill Carr of Pennsylvania, slim and dark-haired against the favourite, tall, blond, bespectacled Ben Eastman of Stanford, current world record holder at 46·4 seconds. Both men left the other four finalists far behind and were neck and neck at the home stretch. Then Carr put in a tremendous finishing burst to win

A skier caught in a blur of speed

Four faces of Emil Zatopek, the superman who always seemed to be on the verge of collapse

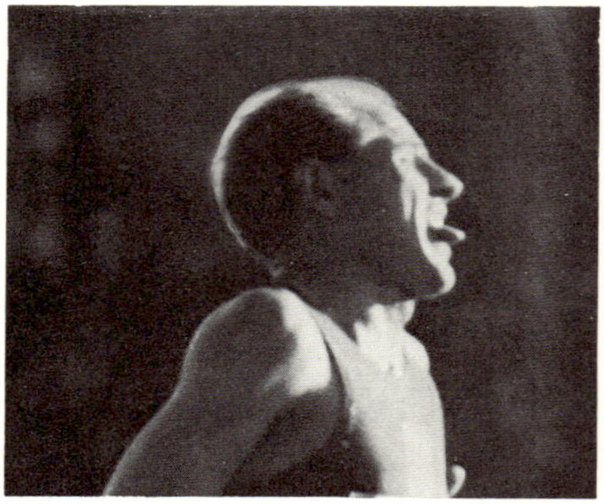

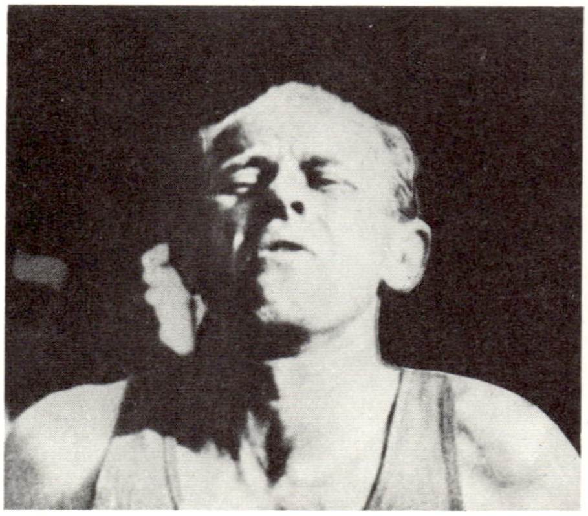

in an amazing time of 46·2 seconds—a new world record. The record stood until after the war with the arrival of the Jamaicans, Herb McKenley and Arthur Wint. Tragically, Carr broke both legs in a car accident in the following year and never had the chance to repeat or improve upon his Olympic performance.

American runners were unplaced in the 800 metres, which was surprisingly won by a bespectacled English schoolmaster named Tom Hampson from Alex Wilson and Phil Edwards of Canada, also in a world record time of 1:49·8. And 39-year-old Tom Green gave Britain another gold medal in the 50 kilometre walk with the popular veteran Ugo Frigerio finishing third. America's George Saling won the 110 metres hurdles in a final in which nearly all the competitors knocked down one or more hurdles (Saling was killed in a car accident in 1933). But Americans were edged out in the 400 metres hurdles by Ireland's Bob Tisdall in the world record time of 51·7 seconds. Finally the American runners set their seal on both relays with easy victories in world record times.

In the field events, genial Dr Pat O'Callaghan retained his crown in the hammer with a tremendous final throw, and America took the long jump, pole vault, shot putt and discus events. Japan's Chuhei Nambu set a new world mark in winning the triple jump, and the powerful American footballer Jim Bauch upset the giant Finn, Akilles Jaervinen to take the decathlon—again with a world record total of points.

Star of the women athletes was America's Mildred (Babe) Didrikson who won two gold medals in the 80 metres hurdles and javelin and a silver in the high jump—undeniably the leading pre-war all-round competitor.

Winding up the highly successful proceedings, as usual, was the Marathon. Leading nearly all the way was the 20-year-old Argentinian Juan Carlos Zabala and in winning from Britain's Sam Ferris he beat Kohlemainen's Antwerp record in a time of 2 hours 31 minutes 36·0 seconds.

The outside events at Los Angeles were also handsomely staged, Boxing, wrestling, fencing, weightlifting and gymnastics were held in a splendid auditorium seating 10,000 spectators. All these events were dominated by the Europeans, especially France, Italy, Germany, Sweden and Hungary. India, as at Amsterdam, proved unbeatable on the hockey field. And in the magnificent swimming pool—which could accommodate 12,000 spectators—records again went by the board in most events, with Japan's talented under-17 swimmers taking four individual gold medals as well as the relay. America's women took six out of seven golds.

When the busy Olympic programme had been completed the medal presentation ceremony took place before a packed stadium, followed by the traditional closing ceremony with the flags of Greece, the United States and Germany (hosts of the next Olympics) flying side by side.

The threatening storm—Berlin 1936

The heavy rain that fell for much of the duration of the 1936 Olympic Games in Berlin might, with hindsight, have been regarded as a baleful symbol of the darkening world scene after the sunny conditions of Los Angeles. Much had happened during those fateful four years, none of it calculated to foster the Olympic ideal of brotherhood and international understanding. In Germany itself Hitler and the Nazis were now firmly in power and determined to turn the XIth Olympics into a national showpiece underlining German supremacy in the sports arena as in other more menacing areas. Meantime Italy had swallowed up tiny Ethiopia, Japan had invaded Manchuria and left the League of Nations, and Spain was on the brink of a civil war which proved to be the prelude to the greater holocaust to come.

Despite these highly unpromising portents the Berlin Games, once the early disputes and problems had been sorted out, proved to be superbly organized and almost entirely trouble-free. In the magnificent new stadium, accommodating 110,000 people, and in eight other splendid arenas, over 4,000 athletes (the largest number yet) from 53 nations entertained almost capacity crowds. In the track and field events five world records and sixteen Olympic records were set and one equalled. And Chancellor Adolf Hitler's cherished creed of Aryan supremacy was demolished by the dazzling successes of the black runners and jumpers from the United States—and one in particular who, in defiance of national and political loyalties, became the

The Olympic Stadium at Helsinki

Alfred Schwarzmann of Germany, who won 3 gold medals for gymnastics in 1936 and subsequently a silver medal at Helsinki, when he was 42 years old

darling of the Berlin crowd, the great Jesse Owens.

The IVth Winter Games had already gone off without a hitch in February at Garmisch-Partenkirchen in the Bavarian Alps, not far from Munich. These attracted about 300 competitors and the pattern was much as in previous years. Sonja Henie won the third and last of her Olympic figure skating titles while Austria's Karl Schafer repeated his 1932 victory. The Germans won the pairs figure skating crown and the amazing Norwegian speed skater Ivar Ballangrud, winner of the 5,000 metres in St Moritz in 1928, took golds in that event as well as in the 500 and 10,000 metre races. The gifted Norwegian Birger Rouud repeated his 1932 victory in the ski-jumping and the remaining skiing events were won by Sweden, Norway and—in the newly introduced slalom events—Germany. The United States and Switzerland shared the bobsled gold medals and Britain's ice hockey team surprisingly defeated both Canada and the United States.

The dilemma facing United States athletes

The Nazi programme of religious persecution, already in full swing, coupled with their widely advertised racialist theories, posed a serious dilemma for many participants in the XIth Olympics, no nation being more directly affected than the United States, with her Jewish and Negro athletes. Eventually, but only by a very close vote, it was decided to send a fully representative team; and although out of the squad of 382 men and women only ten black track and field athletes were included, that handful was to make a public mockery of Nazi ideology and by so doing restore faith in the Olympic values originally outlined by Baron de Coubertin.

The opening of the Games on Saturday August 1, though undeniably impressive, hardly boded well for the cause of international amity. Leading the parade was the legendary Spiridon Louis, winner of the first Marathon, in Greek national dress, bearing a branch of wild olive from Olympia as a gift to the German Chancellor. The teams in political sympathy with the Nazi regime gave the Hitler salute and were warmly applauded. Others, including the British and United States teams, gave the traditional "eyes right" salute and were either received in silence or with jeers and whistles. The home team, bringing up the rear, naturally won a standing ovation. But once the track and field events began on Sunday August 2, the spectators, though pardonably partisan, sat back to enjoy an unparalleled display of sporting entertainment.

The "Ebony Antelope"

The excited spectators had only to wait a short time before they had something to cheer about. The German shot putter Hans Woellke won the first event—and the first gold medal ever won by a German male athlete—to earn a public congratulation by Hitler in his box. The Finns then made a clean sweep of the 10,000 metres and, in fairness, the Chancellor received the winner Ilmari Salminen in the same manner. In the meantime the crowd were given their first glimpse of the much-heralded American athlete, Owens. Owens came to Berlin with an impressive record already behind him. The son of a cotton picker and a student at Ohio University, Owens had met and defeated the cream of the American athletic world, though he had not yet taken the measure of another great Negro sprinter Ralph Metcalfe. Yet the fantastic Owens, nicknamed the "Ebony Antelope" had, at Ann Arbor, Michigan, on the single afternoon of May 25, 1935—to be precise within the space of 70 minutes—won four successive events, setting up five new world records and equalling another. In the 100 yards his official 9·4 seconds equalled the world record but all present agreed it was nearer 9·3 seconds. There was no dispute about the long jump which he won with a prodigious record-breaking leap of 26 feet 8¼ inches (unsurpassed for 25 years). Then he streaked home in the 220 yards sprint in a world record time of 20·3 seconds (being credited with the same time, also a record, for the 200 metres). And to crown the afternoon he set up a similar mark for the 220 yards hurdles (22·6 seconds), valid also for the 200 metres distance. The following month he won a 100 metres final in 10·2 seconds, yet another world record which was to stand for 20 years!

Owens' achievement during the first week in Berlin was as memorable as that afternoon at Ann Arbor, despite the fact that he set no new world marks. On the first Sunday he won his first 100 metres heat in 10·3 and followed it in the quarter final with an amazing 10·2—though the record was not allowed since he was judged to be wind-assisted. Ralph Metcalfe qualified easily as well. But the greatest embarrassment for Hitler came when the Negro Cornelius Johnson cleared 6 feet 7⅞ inches to win the high jump, with his black team-mate Dave Albritton taking the silver. At that point Hitler and his entourage left the stadium, making the excuse that rain was threatening.

A dramatic week

On Monday August 3, a cold, wet

The Olympic downhill course at Cortina, where the 1956 Winter Games were held

day, Owens won his semi-final of the 100 metres in 10·4 and lined up with Ralph Metcalfe for the final. Owens got off to a flying start, Metcalfe a bad one. Metcalfe blazed down the course but just failed to overtake Owens who broke the tape in 10·3, equalling the Olympic record. Hitler made no comment but pointedly abandoned his ceremony of public accolades. Even when the German, Karl Hein won the gold medal for the hammer throw on the same day, Hitler received him in discreet privacy out of the spectators' view. But that damp day was as nothing to the next, labelled by Nazi journalists "Black Tuesday", the day when the so-called "Black Auxiliaries" headed by Owens, really showed their mettle. In the heats of the 200 metres Owens and Mack Robinson cruised to the semi-finals, Robinson equalling the Olympic record of 21·2 and Owens promptly lowering it to 21·1. Then he prepared to qualify for the long jump finals. Unbelievably, he was twice shown the red flag, indicating foul jumps. One leap left and all he needed was a qualifying 23 feet 5½ inches. But he was visibly nervous. His leading German rival Luz Long advised him to move his take-off back. Owens allowed himself a good two feet—and qualified by one-sixteenth of an inch!

In the afternoon Owens, again aided by a stiff breeze, recorded another 21·1 seconds in the 200 metres quarter-finals. Then he ambled over to the scene of his morning near-disaster for the long jump finals. Full of confidence now, he jumped 25 feet 4¾ inches, then 25 feet 9¾ inches. But Luz Long, egged on by thousands of excited supporters, was also in searing form. With his fifth jumps he exactly equalled Owens' leap. Owens

crouched, sprinted, rose high in the air with his familiar hitch-kicking motion, and made a perfect landing —26 feet ½ inch. The German's last jump was a foul and Owens had won his second gold medal, for good measure recording a mighty 26 feet 5¼ inches on his last jump (an Olympic record that stood till 1960).

The relatively unknown Negro runner, Johnny Woodruff, completed Hitler's depressing afternoon by beating Italy's Mario Lanzi on the home stretch of the 800 metres after a hectic run in which he had twice been hemmed in on the inside of the track and forced to make a wide detour to pass his rivals.

On Wednesday August 5, another bleak day, the stands were packed to see Owens try for his third medal, in the 200 metres final. By now he was the darling of the crowd, no matter what their political leanings. And they were well rewarded. His triumph came late in the day, and there was never any doubt of the result as he roared home in an Olympic record time of 20·7 seconds, with Mack Robinson again in second place. The stadium erupted in applause, but Hitler had again sensed bad weather and discreetly departed.

Thursday August 6 saw the Ger-

Spectators at the Games in Innsbruck and Cortina. An unexpected fall of freezing rain had turned the slope leading to the spectators' gallery into a sheet of ice which could only be negotiated with the help of ropes

Toni Sailer, triple gold medalist at Cortina, on the treacherous downhill course

Murray Halberg of New Zealand, who won a gruelling 5,000 metres at the Rome Olympics.

man Gerhard Stoeck win a surprising victory in the javelin throw and a new world record for yet another Japanese triple jumper, Naoto Tajimo. But the event of the day was the thrilling final of the 1,500 metres which brought together the 1932 gold medalist Luigi Beccali, America's world-record miler, Glenn Cunningham, and a red-haired London medical student, New Zealand-born Jack Lovelock. Britain's great miler Sydney Wooderson had disappointingly failed to qualify as a result of an ankle injury. In the home straight it was Lovelock, Cunningham, Beccali, and they finished in that order; Lovelock establishing a world record of 3:37·8.

On the Friday, the 400 metres final was won by yet another Negro athlete, Archie Williams, with Britain's Arthur Brown separating him from Williams' black colleague Jimmy LuValle. And on Saturday Finland's great steeplechaser Volmari Iso-Hollo (third in the 10,000 metres) retained his 1932 crown in winning the 3,000 metres in Olympic record time, while Americans took all the medals in the decathlon.

Only the Marathon and the two relay races were left for the Sunday. Then, to the immense delight of the crowd, the amazing Owens took his fourth gold medal as he anchored the United States team to victory in the 400 metres relay event, again in world record time.

In the 1600 metres relay, Great Britain, inspired by the superb Godfrey Rampling, came through to beat the United States and Germany (Harold Whitlock having won the 50 kilometres walk in Britain's only other track success of the Games). The Marathon, in which Juan Carlos Zabala attempted to repeat his 1932 victory, was unexpectedly won by the Japanese runner Kitei Son, with Britain's Ernest Harper second and another Japanese, Shoryu Nan, third.

It had been a dramatic week. Although the host country had chalked up wins in the field as well as in boxing, cycling, the equestrian events, gymnastics, rowing, canoeing and handball (a new event) there was no doubt that the United States, with twelve golds in the track and field and spearheaded by their gifted black athletes, had carried away the real honours. Doubtless they would all be back in Tokyo in 1940 for the XIIth Olympics. As the flags were lowered over the closing ceremony a week later nobody could have imagined that it would be twelve years before the Olympic flame was lit again. But Hitler himself would see to that.

Games for a tired world— London 1948

The XII and XIIIth Olympics were never held. In 1938 Japan, at war with China, relinquished the right to hold the 1940 Games and handed it over to Finland. But by 1940 Finland had herself been overrun by Russia and Europe was ablaze. The 1948 Games, held in London, were notable for the absence of two of the war-defeated nations, Germany and Japan, and one of the victors, the Soviet Union.

The auguries were not good for the XIVth Olympics. Britain had emerged from the war victorious but sapped of strength. Rationing and austerity were still the order of the day and there seemed to be little popular enthusiasm, much less prior publicity. Furthermore the Winter Olympics at St Moritz earlier in the year had been dogged by uncertain weather, confused organization and international bickering, two rival American ice hockey teams being the main cause of acrimony. After near-cancellation the Games got under way. Popular Dick Button of the USA won the men's figure skating and Barbara Ann Scott took the gold for Canada in the women's event, with the pairs title going to Belgian skaters. Norwegians took three speed skating events, Sweden a fourth. The skiing events now included three for women, one of which was won by America's Gretchen Frazer but the Scandinavian nations, France and Switzerland shared most of the gold medals.

Lord Burghley, 1928 hurdling gold medallist, thus had an unenviable task as head of the British Olympic Association responsible for organizing the Games. Yet the impossible was done. No new building was attempted but Wembley Stadium made a fitting venue for the 6,000 athletes from 59 nations who paraded before King George V on a sun-baked afternoon of July 29. More than 80,000 people watched a spectacular opening, climaxed by the arrival of the Olympic flame, brought across land and sea from Olympia by 1,600 runners in relay. And the following day, still unseasonably hot, saw the first excitement of the meeting in the 10,000 metres.

A victory ceremony at the Winter Olympics in Squaw Valley

Zatopek, the new hero

The favourite for this race was Viljo Heino, world record holder and the last in the great line of Finnish distance runners. Even the experts paid little heed to a shabbily clad, barrel-chested army lieutenant from Czechoslovakia by the name of Emil Zatopek, despite reports of recent near-record times. The field set off as thunderclouds gathered, Heino with a graceful controlled stride, Zatopek with contorted face, rolling head and shoulders, clutching hands—the very antithesis of a classic distance runner. But Zatopek, if no stylist, had unlimited strength and stamina thanks to a self-imposed training programme which stretched his body to the limits. Slightly before the halfway mark he raced past the astonished Heino, who, weary and demoralized soon dropped out of the race. Then as the crowd shouted him on the blond Czech steadily increased his pace as his exhausted rivals fell farther behind or simply gave up. He blazed home in an Olympic record time of 29:59·6, over 300 yards ahead of Mimoun of France.

The sweet smile of success: Valeriy Brumel of the USSR, who won the high jump silver at Rome and (right) *the gold at Tokyo*

The athletic world had discovered a new hero. Three days later Zatopek was in action again in the 5,000 metres final. The weather had turned really grim by now, but a huge crowd braved the murky downpour to see Zatopek trailing until the last lap. Then he sent the crowd wild with excitement as he pounded in pursuit of the Belgian Gaston Reiff, just failing to catch him at the tape—there was only a yard and a fifth of a second in it.

The United States sprinters and hurdlers were in devastating form. The superb Mel Patton nosed out his veteran team-mate, the Negro Barney Ewell in the 200 metres, after Ewell had been narrowly beaten in the 100 metres final by another black athlete, Harrison Dillard. Dillard, whose boyhood hero was Owens, was really a champion hurdler but had failed to qualify for the Olympics and had switched to the sprint—determined to win a gold for something. In the 800 metres the US air force sergeant, Mal Whitfield, broke Tom Hampton's Olympic record with 1:49·2, just edging out the British crowd's favourite, Arthur Wint, the massive Jamaican. But Wint had his moment of glory later in the 400 metres final which he won from another Jamaican, the magnificent quarter-miler Herb McKenley.

The war, and subsequent disqualifications from amateur ranks, deprived the spectators of a sight of the two great runners from Sweden who had progressively broken all records for the mile and the 1,500 metres—Gunder Hägg and Arne Andersson. But two other Swedes— Henry Eriksson and Lennart Strand still took the gold and silver for the 1,500 finals at the London Games. Sweden also took all three places in the 3,000 metres steeplechase, and two more golds in the 10 kilometre and 50 kilometre walks.

There were more thrills in the field events as the Australian, John Winter, despite a back injury, won the high jump from the favoured Americans, and Hungary's Imre Nemeth took the hammer throw. The great Italian discus thrower Adolfo Consolini—who had competed as a teenager in Berlin, held the world record twice, and was still breaking the European record for 1955 when almost forty—took the gold in that event. The pole vault was won by America's Guinn Smith at 14 feet $1\frac{1}{4}$ inches. The greatest pole vaulter in the world, also from the USA—Cornelius

666

Peter Snell, the first middle-distance runner to win three Olympic gold medals

Warmerdam, who had been the first man to clear 15 feet, had now retired, prevented by war from appearing in the Olympics. He had set up world records of 15 ft $7\frac{3}{4}$ in. outdoors and 15 ft $8\frac{1}{2}$ in. indoors.

Two outstanding all-rounders

Of the United States golds, none was more deserved than that won by Bob Mathias, a massively built seventeen-year-old who won the decathlon in absolutely appalling weather conditions—an exploit rivalling that of Jim Thorpe himself. Meanwhile a thirty-year-old Dutch housewife named Fanny Blankers-Koen was carving out another piece of Olympic history by romping off with no less than four gold medals—in the 100 metre and 200 metre sprints, the 80 metre hurdles, and as the anchor leg in the 400 metres relay. Had she entered for the high jump and long jump as well, she might easily have collected six—she happened to be the world record holder for both events at the time.

There was a last-day drama in the Marathon—reminiscent of Pietri's despairing effort in the 1908 London Games. First into the stadium after the two-way trek out to Radlett and back to Wembley was the Belgian, Etienne Gailly. But the effort had exhausted him and as he staggered, barely conscious, round the last lap of the track he was overtaken, first by Delfo Cabrera of the Argentine—who took the gold—then by the British runner Tom Richards. Gailly just managed to stagger over the line for the bronze and was carried off on a stretcher.

The "Zatopek Games"— Helsinki 1952

When remembering Helsinki it is difficult to think of it as the setting for the XVth Olympics; rather the memory makes a leap to the name which dominated the proceedings, and Helsinki becomes in the mind's eye the setting for the "Zatopek Games". No single Olympics has been dominated by an individual in the way that the 1952 Games were by Emil Zatopek, and as if it were not enough to have probably the greatest distance runner the world has seen at the height of his powers, there was another gold-winning Zatopek, his wife Dana. This, of course, should not belittle the other 4,923 individuals, representing the athletic prowess of 69 nations, who came to the Finnish capital and contained among their number many outstanding competitors. But the impression of Zatopek lingers longest, not only for the medals he achieved but also for the rhythmic chanting of his name which the Finnish crowds took up as he stormed round the last lap towards each of his memorable triumphs. And no country loves a distance runner better than the Finns, who have themselves provided so many fine exponents of the art. It was somehow appropriate that, in the beautiful stadium at Helsinki, the

Sixten Jernberg, the great Swedish cross-country skier. In three Olympics he won a total of nine medals

honours should be won by a runner in the great tradition of men such as Kolehmainen, Ritola, Lehtinen and Nurmi.

Before the Summer gathering, Norway had at last won its claim to stage a Winter Olympics, though they were embarrassed by an almost unknown phenomenon in that country in February—a relative shortage of snow. Despite this, the Games went off smoothly, the Norwegians were exceptionally hospitable hosts, and the popularity of the winter half of the Olympic programme was confirmed beyond doubt. Thirty nations competed, and a total of 750,000 people watched them, most of them no doubt happy at the successes achieved by the home nation. Norway won the men's giant slalom, the 15 kilometres cross-country, the Nordic combined jump and cross-country, and, best of all, she produced the winner of the four speed skating competitions, Hjalmar Andersen. There was also a satisfying climax to the ski-jumping staged at Holmenkillen: this attracted huge crowds which saw the Norwegian Arnfinn Bergmann emerge with the gold. An American girl, Andrea Lawrence-Mead, won both the slalom and the giant slalom, and the German Annemarie Buchner collected two bronzes and a silver in the Alpine skiing. The United States also produced the winner of the men's figure skating, Richard Button taking the gold for the second successive Olympics with that combination of daring and agility which other competitors were still a long way from achieving. In the women's figure skating, Jeanette Altwegg became the first British skater ever to win an Olympic title.

The Soviet Union competes once more

When the Summer Olympics came to Helsinki, there was one notable addition to the list of competing countries—the Soviet Union was represented once again after an absence of forty years. They made no great mark on these Games, except with the might of their formidable lady throwers, but it was no doubt a satisfying testing ground for the impression they intended to make in future Olympics. In Helsinki, the Americans were still kings of the medals table with the immensely versatile array of talent that they habitually produced for the Games. In the 100 metres they were perhaps lucky to come out with the gold, a tremendously exciting race bringing the crowd out of their seats as four men seemed to burst through the tape in the same instant. An intensive study of the photo-finish eventually produced the following medal winners—gold, Lindy Remigino (USA); silver, Herb McKenley (Jamaica); bronze, E. McDonald Bailey (Great Britain). The time was 10·4 seconds.

McKenley took the silver also in the 400 metres, which was won by his compatriot, George Rhoden, in

At Tokyo, Don Schollander of the USA became the first man to win four swimming golds at a Games

Eero Maentyranta of Finland, one of Jernberg's great rivals

the record time of 45·9 seconds. Arthur Wint had won this event in 1948, so it meant that a Jamaican tradition was maintained, and, not surprisingly, the relay team of McKenley, Rhoden, Wint and Laing carried off the 1600 metres in great style, setting a new record of 3 minutes 3·9 seconds. Wint was again in the medals in the 800 metres, this race finishing in almost identical manner to the race in the London Olympics, Mal Whitfield repeating his success and recording exactly the same time, Wint one-tenth of a second faster than he had been in 1948, but still having to be content with the silver.

The water in an Olympic swimming pool is not just ordinary water—salt is added to give the swimmers greater buoyancy and chemicals allow them to glide along more easily through the water

The United States had the first three in the 200 metres, Andy Stanfield winning in a new record of 20·7 seconds, and the first three in the 110 metres hurdles. In the latter, Harrison Dillard won in a record 13·7 seconds and achieved the unique distinction of golds in two completely diverse events. In London he had won the 100 metres by sheer determination, almost in anger because he had slipped up in the US qualifying competition for the Olympic 110 metres hurdles. Now he competed in his rightful event and finally proved his superiority, though the outcome between Jack Davis and him was always in doubt, both being given the same time.

Australia came to the fore in the women's sprints, Marjorie Jackson bringing off a resounding double in the 100 metres and 200 metres, both in record-breaking times. Shirley Strickland also collected the bronze in the 100 metres and won the 80 metres hurdles, another new record. With such sprinting strength it was almost inevitable that Australia would win the 4 × 100 metres relay, and they became hot favourites when they set a new Olympic record of 46·1 seconds in the preliminaries. But sadly, in the final they dropped the baton, and the title went to the United States, who lowered the record once more to 45·9 seconds.

First gold for Luxemburg

In the 1,500 metres, diminutive Luxemburg won its first gold medal, Josef Barthel outpacing Robert McMillen of the United States, and recording a new Olympic best of 3 minutes 45·1 seconds. (This 1,500 metres field included Roger

Bannister, but it was to be another two years before he was to win immortality in the record books with the first sub-four-minute mile). If it was unique in 1952 for Luxemburg to win an Olympic gold of any kind, it was also unique for the United States to win a distance race. Far back in 1904 and 1908, that country had provided the winners of the Marathon, but since then no American had won a gold, and the 5,000 metres, 10,000 metres and 3,000 metres steeplechase had never gone outside Europe for their victors. It was against the form book that the USA won the steeplechase in Helsinki, but all credit must be given to Horace Ashenfelter who showed great tenacity in holding off Kazantsev of the Soviet Union and finally beating him, winning by more than 6 seconds in a new record. Another American, Bob Mathias, showed invincible all-round athletic gifts in retaining his decathlon title, amassing a new record total of 7,887 points.

Records tumbled in the women's long jump, in the men's high jump, and in the triple jump. In the first, Yvette Williams cleared 20 feet $5\frac{3}{4}$ inches and confirmed the feeling that New Zealand's star was in the ascendant in international athletics. In the high jump the American, Walter Davis won the gold at 6 feet $8\frac{3}{8}$ inches, and in the triple jump, Adhemar Ferreira da Silva of Brazil proved that a long name is no handicap to being airborne, recording 53 feet $2\frac{1}{2}$ inches. Records likewise came to be commonplace in the throwing events, in which the Americans collected three gold medals, one of them for the javelin, and again this was the first time a non-European had won it. The American hero in this case was Cy Young, who threw 242 feet $\frac{1}{2}$ inch. Parry O'Brien won the shot, Simeon Iness the discus, but Hungary managed to retain the hammer title. In the women's events the Russians grabbed the shot and the discus golds, as they would continue to do in almost unbroken sequence down the years.

In the swimming pool the dominance of the United States was only slightly less total than in 1948. In the women's events, in particular, the Hungarians stole a march on them, winning four golds, and America's only female successes belonged to Pat McCormick in the two diving events. In the boxing

Willi Holdorf of Germany collapsed at the finishing line, but still won the 1964 gold medal in the decathlon

ring, Laszlo Papp, also of Hungary, won his second gold medal, this time at light middleweight. The middleweight champion was Floyd Patterson. In the Grand Prix jumping, the British team won the gold medal, and on the soccer field the Hungarians were champions, with a team that contained such names as Puskas, Hidegkuti, Kocsis, Grosics, names that would echo round the temples of football within a year.

The Czech locomotive

What then of the Zatopeks? In cold statistics, Emil won an unprecedented treble of golds, in the process taking 11 seconds off the 5,000 metres record, 42·6 seconds off his own 10,000 metres Olympic record, and running the Marathon over 6 minutes faster than it had ever been run before. On the same day that he won the 5,000 metres, his wife Dana won the gold medal for the javelin and this, he said, gave him more satisfaction than any of his own triumphs. The 10,000 metres was predictably his after the devastating way he had come to the world's notice in winning this race in 1948. Only the little Algerian Mimoun, running in the colours of France, presented any threat, but once again he could not keep up with the pace of the relentless Czech and was 90 yards behind when Zatopek broke the tape in 29 minutes 17·0 seconds. The 5,000 metres was a different matter—Zatopek was not a sprinter, and he had let the Belgian, Reiff, run away from him in London. The field in Helsinki was exceptionally strong, with Reiff, Schade of Germany, Mimoun, and the young Chataway of Great Britain all possible winners. Schade seemed anxious to set the pace, and with 1,000 metres to go he still led from Zatopek and Reiff. Astonishingly, on the penultimate lap, Reiff quit, leaving four runners in contention at the bell—Schade, Zatopek, Chataway and Mimoun. Zatopek made a bid for the lead but was overtaken by Chataway, then by Schade and Mimoun, all sprinting away from him down the back straight. The panting Czech athlete looked really short of steam as the other runners showed him their heels. It looked as though he would be out of the medals altogether. But coming into the final bend he produced one of those magnificent, agonizing, ungainly, and immensely courageous efforts which so much endeared him to the crowds and which against all the probabilities won him the race. He ran out into the third lane, overtook Schade, was bumped by Mimoun, recovered, drew level with Mimoun and Chataway, and just pulled clear. The luckless Chataway tripped and fell, the race became a sprint for the tape between the three runners, and to the crowd's delirious excitement, Zatopek held the lead in the home stretch, heaving himself towards the line with Mimoun and Schade following in his wake. They finished in that order. It has often been described as the "race of the century".

Zatopek, however, had yet another surprise in store. He had never run in the Marathon or even an equivalent distance, did not know how to train for it, and when he lined up for the start had really no idea what sort of pace to maintain. After 10,000 metres he was comfortably up at the front behind Jim Peters; after 25,000 metres he found he was still feeling strong and running with Jansson, the Swede, ahead of the field; after 30,000 he was alone and nobody was left to run with him. By the time he reached the stadium his chest was heaving and his limbs were only wearily going through their motions, but he was 2½ minutes clear of any challenger and the crowd had risen to him, chanting, all of them, "Zatopek, Zatopek, Zatopek!"

The XVIth Olympics—Melbourne 1956

The XVIth Olympics were held in the unusual months of November and December, the reason being that the Games had come to the Southern Hemisphere for the first time and were held at the height of the Australian summer. The number of competitors was slightly lower than at Helsinki, but this was to be expected considering the seasonal difficulties and the great distances involved for many nations. The only events that could not be held in Australia were the equestrian ones; because of strict quarantine laws in that country these competitions took place in Stockholm. Overall, the Melbourne Games were highly successful and very well attended by the Australian public, who had the pleasure of seeing their own competitors bring in a good haul of medals.

Nine months before the Olympic torch burned beneath the Australian sky, the Winter Games were staged in the majestic setting of the Dolomites, at the Italian ski resort of Cortina d'Ampezzo. A record number of 947 competitors representing some 32 nations participated, and the Italians reputedly spent some $7,500,000 on the organization of the Games. For the first time, the Soviet Union was represented and collected an impressive tally of golds, winning two of the cross-country races, three of the four speed-skating events, and the ice hockey. But this prolific national debut in the Winter Sports was overshadowed by the achievement of a 20-year-old Austrian, Toni Sailer, who became the first man to win all three gold medals in the Alpine skiing. Each of his victories was by a convincing margin, and he startled onlookers with the audacity of his skiing on what was for many competitors a treacherous course (particularly the downhill), and which he conquered with ease. In the cross-country skiing Sixten Jernberg of Sweden won two individual silvers and a gold, and shared a bronze for the relay. He had some notable battles with the great Finn, Veikko Hakulinen, who won a gold and two silvers. The men's figure skating was monopolized by the Americans, Hayes Jenkins, Ronald Robertson and David Jenkins being awarded the medals in that order. The United States also supplied

The opening of the Winter Olympics in Grenoble. French paratroopers land in the Olympic stadium, right on the target—the five-ringed Olympic symbol

the first two in the women's figure skating in the persons of Tenley Albright and Carol Heiss. Austria won the bronze and the Austrian pair, Elisabeth Schwarz and Kurt Oppelt, were victorious in the pairs event. The Italians provided the gold and silver medalists in the two-man bobsleigh, and the silver medalists in the four-man, which the Swiss won.

Australian swimmers triumph

In many ways, the Summer Games in Melbourne followed patterns set in Helsinki four years earlier, the major reverse being the swimming events in which, to the delight of the home crowds, the Australians gave the Americans an old-fashioned drubbing, winning eight gold medals. Australia had the first three in the men's 100 metres freestyle, setting a new record time, and the individual winner of the 400 metres and 1,500 metres, Murray Rose, who broke the record in each, reducing the longer race time by the remarkable margin of 31·1 seconds. In the 800 metres freestyle relay Australia led the Americans home by almost 8 seconds. Another

Australian, David Theile, won the 100 metres backstroke, and in the women's events two more home-grown stars emerged—Dawn Fraser in the 100 metres, setting a new record of 1 minute 2·0 seconds, and Lorraine Crapp in the 400 metres, who chopped 15½ seconds off the previous best time. Predictably, these two helped Australia to another gold in the freestyle relay. The United States could only salvage the two butterfly events, the men's springboard diving, and the two women's diving competitions in which the admirable Pat McCormick repeated her double success of Helsinki. Britain had one splendid victor in Judy Grinham who swam the 100 metres backstroke in the record-breaking time of 1 minute 12·9 seconds.

It was on the track, in the sprint events, that the 1952 results were chiefly duplicated, the United States monopolizing the men's events, Australia the women's. Both countries produced triple gold medalists in Bobby-Joe Morrow and Betty Cuthbert. Morrow won the 100 metres, the 200 metres, in which he lowered the record to 20·6 seconds, and was anchor-man in the 400 metres relay which the United States won. He was a strong candidate to break the record in the 100 metres, as he had equalled it in the heats, but the final was run into a very stiff wind and his winning time of 10·5 was outstanding in the circumstances. Betty Cuthbert showed herself to be a more than worthy successor to her compatriot Marjorie Jackson by equalling the latter's Helsinki record in the 100 metres and cutting three-tenths of a second off her 200 metres record. With Shirley Strickland, who once again won the 80 metres hurdles, lowering her own record to 10·7 seconds, Australia had the basis of a formidable relay team, and they duly won the gold which they had deserved in Helsinki but had lost by dropping

Striking graphic designs portraying the separate events of the Winter Olympics

Jean-Claude Killy, "king of the ski slopes" in 1968 (left), *and his great rival, Karl Schranz* (right)

Jean-Claude Killy competing in the giant slalom at Grenoble

Gymnasts loosening up before the competition

the baton. Here in Melbourne they produced a record-breaking time, though the race had an exciting finish with Britain and the United States hard on the Australians' heels, and all of them within the former Olympic record.

Both the men's hurdling events were won by the United States, Lee Calhoun taking the 100 metres and Glenn Davis the 400 metres, both setting new records. Poor Jack Davis once again had to be content with the silver in the 100 metres, and once again he was awarded the same time as the winner. He was, therefore, twice a record-breaker and never a gold medalist. The flat 400 metres was also won by an American, Charles Jenkins, but this race was unique in that it provided the only dead-heat for a medal in Olympic track history, Hellsten of Finland and Ignatyev of the USSR tying for the bronze.

There was an exciting finish to the 800 metres with Tom Courtney (USA) just ahead of the British runner Derek Johnson. The time was a record 1 minute 47·7 seconds, and Courtney won a second gold anchoring the 1600 metres relay. The 1,500 metres, however, was something of an anticlimax for the Australians who had hoped to see their own John Landy, current world record holder at the distance, bring home the gold. The time was exceptionally fast, and eight of the twelve finalists finished inside the Olympic record, but the gold went to Ron Delany of Ireland, and Landy was beaten into third position by Richtzenhain of Germany. Delany's time was 3 minutes 41·2 seconds.

Kuts versus Pirie

As in Helsinki, the distance races of 5,000 and 10,000 metres in Melbourne were, so to speak, the Blue Riband events of the Games, and both golds went once again to one man, another champion in the great tradition of distance runners which the Olympics have honoured. His name was Vladimir Kuts, a tough 29-year-old Russian from the Ukraine, who seemed to run on a mixture of sheer strength and will-power. By the time of the Games he was world record holder at 10,000 metres, and only second to Gordon Pirie in 5,000 metre times. The two races promised to be a terrific contest between these two, and it

Mexico City: policewomen guard the entrance to the women athletes' quarters

Opposite: *The marvellous Czech gymnast, Vera Caslavska, on the bar, and later being feted after her victory.*

was well known that neither of them was interested in coming second. For 20 laps in the 10,000 metres, Pirie shadowed Kuts, with the Russian following a policy of running away in surging bursts, trying to break the opposition with a killing pace over the first half of the race so that he would be out on his own for the last stages. Consequently, they were within a fraction of a second of breaking Zatopek's 5,000 metres record as they passed the halfway mark. But Kuts' tactics paid off, for only he could sustain the effort. Pirie was beaten by having to keep up with the sudden sprints, and 2,000 metres from home he fell away. Kuts ran on and on to win by nearly 7 seconds from Kovacs of

A close-up of the "Fosbury Flop"

Hungary, and his time of 28 minutes 45·6 seconds was more than half a minute inside Zatopek's Olympic record. After this it was a foregone conclusion that the 5,000 metres record would fall, and it did, by 27 seconds. In the end the blond head of Kuts was way out in front, some 11 seconds ahead of Pirie, who won the silver. Another British runner, Derek Ibbotson, collected the bronze, and the winning time was 13 minutes 39·6 seconds. Such are the strides made each year in athletics, that record times are reduced by almost absurd margins. After Melbourne no longer would the winning times of the 10,000 and 5,000 metres be prefaced by 29 minutes and 14 minutes; they would start to move down through the seconds following prefixes of 28 minutes and 13 minutes.

Britain did, however, succeed in collecting one track gold, a quite unexpected one in the 3,000 metres steeplechase. The hot favourite was Sandor Rozsnyoi of Hungary, but a splendidly determined run by Christopher Brasher won him the prize in a new record of 8 minutes 41·2 seconds.

Objections sportingly overruled

The jubilation of victory was slightly marred by a controversy in which Brasher found that he had been disqualified for interfering with one of the other runners in the final stages, but Rozsnyoi and Larsen (Norway), who had finished second and third respectively, sportingly claimed that any interference had been purely accidental and had not affected the result. Brasher was reinstated as the winner. It was a magnificent vindication that the Olympic ideals were not dead.

New records were set in the men's high jump, in which Charles Dumas of the United States finished just half an inch short of 7 feet, and in the pole vault, in which Robert Richards, also of the USA, finished just half an inch short of 15 feet. Owens' 1936 long jump record, however, remained untouched, Gregory Bell (USA) winning the gold medal some 9 inches short of it. Adhemar Ferreira da Silva won a gold for the second time in the triple jump, breaking his own record, and new records were also created in both the women's jumping events. As usual in the throwing events, records fell with monotonous regularity; in fact every single event produced a new one. O'Brien won his second gold at the shot, Al Oerter his first at the discus, Harold Connolly won a see-saw battle in the hammer, finally out-throwing the Russian Krivonosov by a mere 6 inches. This was the first time the United States had won this event since their string of victories in the early years of the century. A Norwegian, Egil Danielsen, created a sensation by hurling the javelin a distance of 281 feet 2½ inches, almost 40 feet further than Cy Young's winning throw in 1952. The three throwing events in the

Sensation in the Mexico City Olympic stadium: Fosbury jumps!

women's competitions also produced records that advanced on their predecessors by impressive distances.

Miscellaneous successes in these Melbourne Olympics included the gold, silver and bronze won by the Russians for the new walking event introduced over 20 kilometres. Laszlo Papp, the Hungarian, became the first boxer to win three gold medals when he once more took the

light middleweight title. For Britain Dick McTaggart won a gold at lightweight, and the diminutive but plucky Terry Spinks battled his way to a gold in the flyweight division. Britain also won her first ever fencing gold when Gillian Sheen captured the women's foil. In the men's foil Christian d'Oriola of France, who won the silver medal in 1948 and the gold in 1952, won the gold yet again. Meanwhile, in Stockholm, Britain's horse-riding team won the three-day event, while here in Melbourne the Australian riders of the less temperamental bicycle showed that their invasion of the medals in Helsinki had been no fluke as they again disrupted the habitual European monopoly of this sport.

In the last and toughest event of all, the Marathon, victory went at last to a man who had struggled for so long in the shadow of another. The great Czech competitor, Emil Zatopek, was once more participating in this race, but he had recently undergone an operation, he had never competed in real heat, and the temperature was up into the eighties the day it was run. Consequently the stadium did not see his famous rolling stride appear first of all; instead it welcomed the appearance of little Alain Mimoun, the French Algerian, runner-up to Zatopek in so many races of varying length in the past. Zatopek was sixth, and at thirty-four years of age knew it was his last Olympics. He graciously congratulated the tenacious Mimoun and made his exit. Australia had witnessed only the embers of the fire that had blazed so fiercely in London and Helsinki.

Mexico City: the Olympic rings—symbol of the union of athletes from all five continents

Opposite: *Bob Beamon outjumps all the competitors . . . even the 1964 Olympic champion, Lynn Davies*

The opening ceremony of the 1964 Winter Olympics inthe Bergisel stadium, Innsbruck

CHAPTER 4

THE GAMES OF THE SIXTIES

In many ways the Roman Games were the most perfect of the modern Olympics. Held in late August and early September, the sun poured like molten gold from the sky and this, in the classical setting of the Eternal City, produced a feeling of closeness to the spirit of the ancient Games of Olympia.

But, before the sun of the south, the snows of the far west. The VIIIth Winter Olympics were held at Squaw Valley, California, and a sense of fantasy surrounded them in that the ceremonial arrangements were under the supervision of Walt Disney. On the opening day, shortly before the proceedings proper began, the foul weather of blinding snow and howling wind which had persisted for weeks, miraculously cleared and the sun shone thereafter for the duration of the Games. It was as though Mr Disney had waved his wand.

The sun shone relatively benignly on the North American competitors, too. The United States won two golds and a bronze in the individual figure skating events, picked up three silvers and a bronze in Alpine skiing, one silver at speed skating, and took the bronze in the pairs figure skating, for which Canada won the gold. Canada also won a gold in the women's slalom and a bronze in the men's figure skating, but was surprisingly beaten in the ice hockey by the United States. Probably the most dramatic event of the Winter Games was the 10,000 metres speed skating, in which Kurt Johannesen of Norway broke the world record by a margin of 46 seconds, and in the process took four others with him through the world record barrier, seven others through the Olympic record, and eleven others through their own national records. In the women's speed skating the Russian Lydia Skoblikova showed formidable promise of greater things to come by winning two gold medals, and setting a new world record in the 1,500 metres. A German, Jörgl Thoma, surprisingly won the Nordic Combined event, the first time ever that the Scandinavian stranglehold on this event had been broken. Finally, the veteran Sixten Jernberg refused to leave glory to younger limbs in the cross-country races, and stole off with a gold and a silver.

A gold for Italy

Of the Summer Olympics it could be said that no one competitor dominated the Games but that several contributed to them in a very great way. Some of the individual races stand out like beacons in the night, and there were record times that made even the most shock-hardened journalists blink in

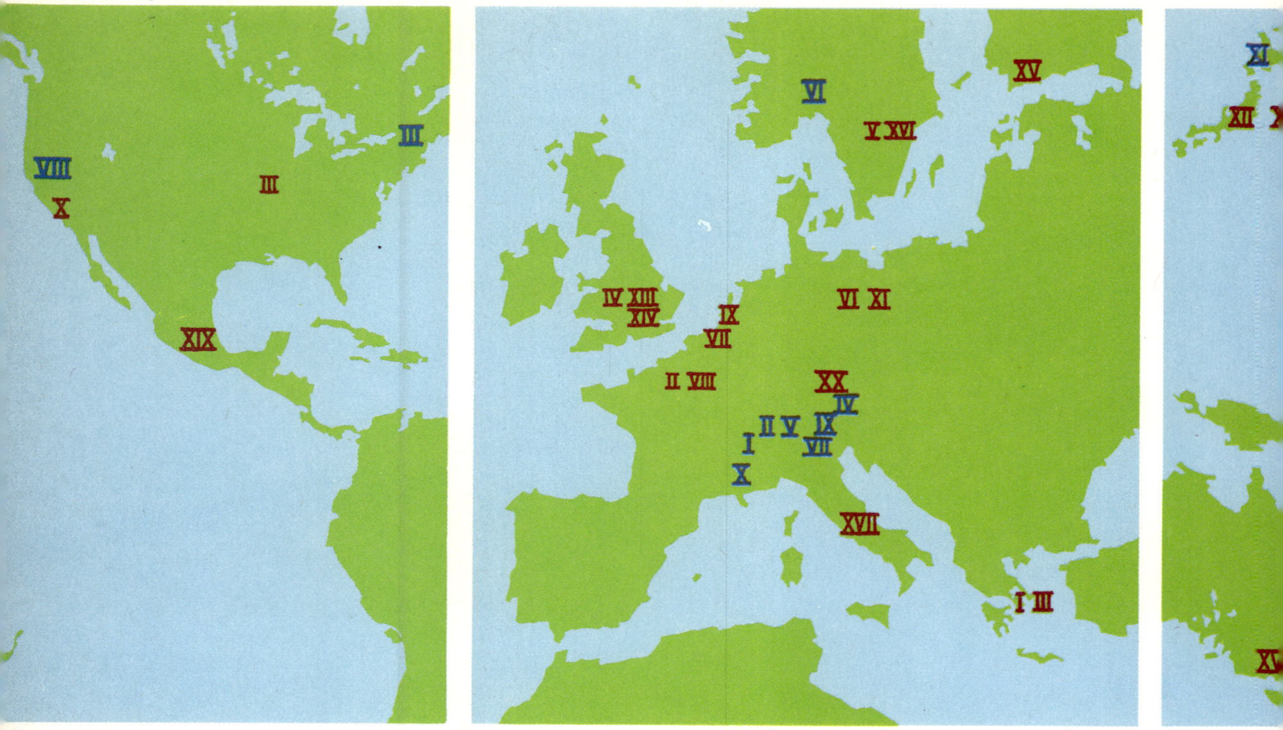

Where the Games have been held:

SUMMER OLYMPICS (in red)—**I** *Athens, 1896;* **II** *Paris, 1900;* **III** *St Louis, 1904;* **IV** *London, 1908;* **V** *Stockholm, 1912;* **VI** *Berlin, 1916* (not held)*;* **VII** *Antwerp, 1920;* **VIII** *Paris, 1924;* **IX** *Amsterdam, 1928;* **X** *Los Angeles, 1932;* **XI** *Berlin, 1936;* **XII** *Tokyo, 1940* (not held)*;* **XIII** *London, 1944* (not held)*;* **XIV** *London, 1948;* **XV** *Helsinki, 1952;* **XVI** *Melbourne, 1956;* **XVII** *Rome, 1960;* **XVIII** *Tokyo, 1964;* **XIX** *Mexico City, 1968;* **XX** *Munich, 1972.*
WINTER OLYMPICS (in blue)—**I** *Chamonix, 1924;* **II** *St Moritz, 1928;* **III** *Lake Placid, 1932;* **IV** *Garmisch-Partenkirchen, 1936;* **V** *St Moritz, 1948;* **VI** *Oslo, 1952;* **VII** *Cortina d'Ampezzo, 1956;* **VIII** *Squaw Valley, 1960;* **IX** *Innsbruck, 1964;* **X** *Grenoble, 1968;* **XI** *Sapporo, 1972.*

Modern architecture for the Olympic Games: the large ice stadium in Grenoble, the "Palazzetto" in Rome and the basketball hall in Mexico City

disbelief. With the sun-soaked setting of the Olympic stadium and the emotional support of the Italian crowds, the whole proceedings had a theatrical air, and it was not surprising that the athletes rose to the occasion and made sport for the Romans. For these last, the greatest sport was made in the 200 metres. A certain amount of excitement had been generated when a dark-haired chemistry student from Turin named Livio Berruti had equalled the world record of 20·5 seconds in the semi-final. But probably they did not believe he could win in the final, Olympic finals being the record-breaking events that they usually are and with three crack Americans in the field. Italy, after all, had never won a major Olympic title. As the runners came round the bend in the final, however, the Italians rose from their seats for there was Berruti in the lead, running with the grace and swiftness of a gazelle, a lead which he held till the tape as the crowd went berserk and made Olympic torches from their newspapers. He had run 20·5 seconds for the second time that afternoon and carried off the gold.

A European also won the 100 metres, and as the Americans were later disqualified from the 400 metres relay (in which they had come first), it was a disastrous Olympics for them as far as the men's sprints were concerned. Armin Hary, the extremely confident German, currently credited with the world record of 10·0 seconds, made good use of his famous fast start and won in 10·2 seconds. Dave Sime of the United States won the silver, and Peter Radford of Great Britain, who was hampered by a slow start, picked up well to claim the bronze. The surprise was that Ray Norton, who had been one of the favourites for the 100 and 200 metres, came away empty-handed. The disqualification from the relay just compounded his disappointment.

The final of the 400 metres was perhaps the most remarkable of all. The American, Otis Davis, surged away down the back straight as if fired from a gun and maintained his momentum until the home stretch where his head went back and he could be seen to be tiring. The German Kaufmann, put in an amazing finishing burst in which he closed yard by yard on Davis and plunged headlong through the tape. Davis, however, was given the verdict in a very close photo-finish, and both runners were given the staggering time of 44·9 seconds, easily a world record.

Another Davis, Glenn, took the gold again in the 400 metres hurdles in the record time of 49·3. In fact the United States had all three medals in this event, as they did in the 110 metres hurdles which Lee Calhoun just won from Willie May. This was compensation for their failures in the sprints, and the women's events brought further rewards, mostly in

The atmosphere of the competition areas and living quarters can have a considerable effect on the athletes' performances. These pictures show the large ice stadium in Squaw Valley, the Campo di Siena show-jumping arena in the Villa Borghese, Rome, and the gaily lighted entrance to the Olympic Village and the fencing hall in Mexico City

the person of Wilma Rudolph, the star of these games if anyone was. A tall, leggy girl from Tennessee, she set a new Olympic record of 11·3 seconds in the heats of the 100 metres, and lowered this again to 11·0 seconds in the final, though this was ruled to have been wind-assisted. With Betty Cuthbert surprisingly eliminated, Rudolph was out on her own in this race, pouring across the ground with incredible facility. Dorothy Hyman of Great Britain ran with great spirit to collect the silver. In the 200 metres, Rudolph again broke the record in the heats, and though the final was slower she was two-fifths of a second ahead of Jutta Heine (Germany) and seven-tenths ahead of Hyman, who finished third. As a journalist who was present later remarked, there was a certain nice irony about the finishing order of the 200 metres. Wilma Rudolph, the black girl, seventeenth child out of nineteen from a poor family in Tennessee, was followed to the tape by Heine, daughter of a German millionaire, and then by Dorothy Hyman, daughter of a Yorkshire miner. It

gave some hope to the Olympic ideal of all people participating in fair and equal competition. Finally, Rudolph showed her real class in the 400 metres relay where she was yards behind as she set out on the last leg but made it up, and collected her third gold of the Games.

Stars from the Antipodes

A new star appeared in the firmament of middle-distance running at Rome. As the runners lined up for the final of the 800 metres, not many eyes paused to consider the figure in the black vest with the silver fern of New Zealand on the front. The favourite was the world record holder, Roger Moens of Belgium, and halfway round the second lap he seemed to have the gold medal in his pocket as he sprinted away, with Kerr of the West Indies and Schmidt of Germany in optimistic pursuit. But in the home straight Moens' stride shortened, the other two

The Miyanomori ski-jump at Sapporo, Japan, site of the Winter Games in 1972

The Makomanai ice stadium at Sapporo

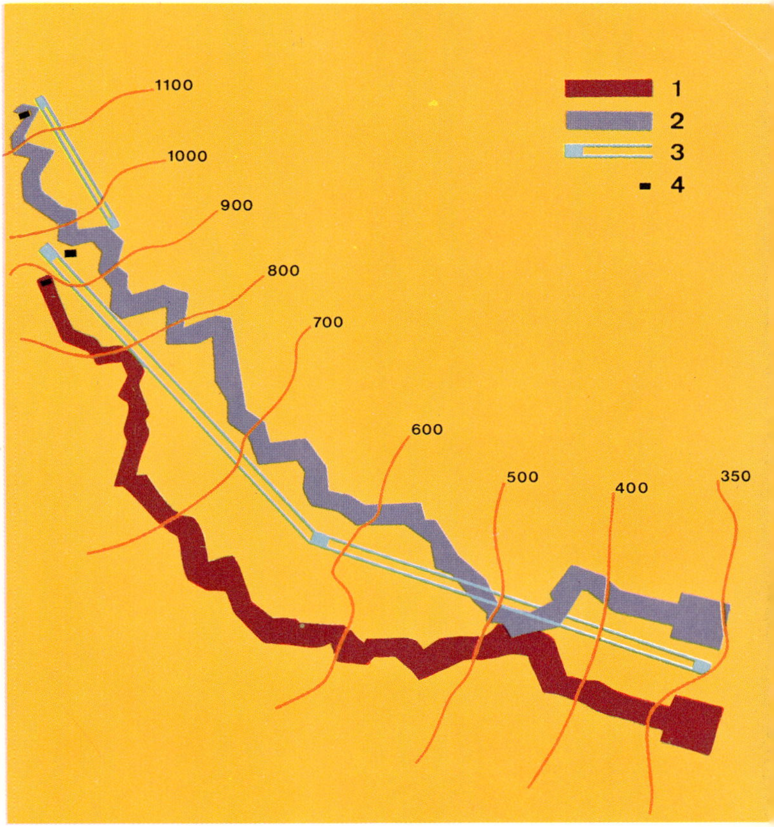

Mt Eniwa, near Sapporo, with the downhill courses cleared of trees:
1 *men's downhill;*
2 *women's downhill;*
3 *cable car;* **4** *refuge and starting huts*

stayed bunched behind him, and the unnoticed Peter Snell slipped through on the inside, opening out into that superb muscular rhythm which was to become so famous, and burst through the tape in a new Olympic record of 1 minute 46·3 seconds. It was hard to believe that Snell's name had been first heard of just six months previously when he had beaten the Australians, Herb Elliott and Tony Blue over 800 metres. The world would hear plenty of it in the years to come.

As for Elliott, he really proved his greatness. Never yet beaten over 1,500 metres, he showed from the outset that he never intended to be, setting the fastest time in the heats and then in the final placing himself comfortably behind the leaders for the first $2\frac{1}{2}$ laps. Coming up to the bell he edged in front, seemingly coasted round the bend, and then kicked away. The rest (all but one sub-four-minute milers, or the equivalent over 1,500 metres) were beaten. Herb Elliott simply ran away from them, pushing that long lean figure to the gold the Australian

Thick snow near Sapporo. A Japanese publicity photograph for the Winter Olympics

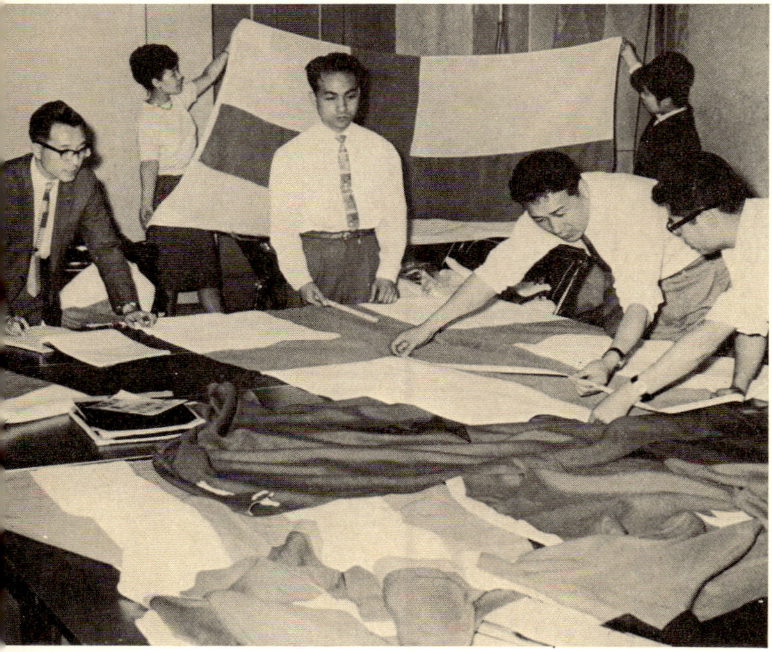

had dreamed of ever since he saw Kuts destroy the 10,000 metres field in Melbourne. All alone at the tape, his time was 3 minutes 35·6 seconds, a new world and Olympic record, two-fifths of a second faster than his previous world record.

Another lean and hungry runner from the Antipodes was the hero of the 5,000 metres, and seldom has a man worked harder for a gold medal. Murray Halberg of New Zealand is much tougher than he looks, a withered arm which resulted from a rugby injury deceptively exaggerating his somewhat emaciated appearance. Like his muscular compatriot, Snell, he had been trained by that great coach Arthur Lydiard; in fact they had trained together, and it must have been an immense satisfaction to all three of them that their efforts produced the two golds they sought. The final of the 5,000 metres was run on an exceptionally hot evening, and the line up, sadly for Britain, showed the absence of both Gordon Pirie and Bruce Tulloh, disappointingly eliminated in the

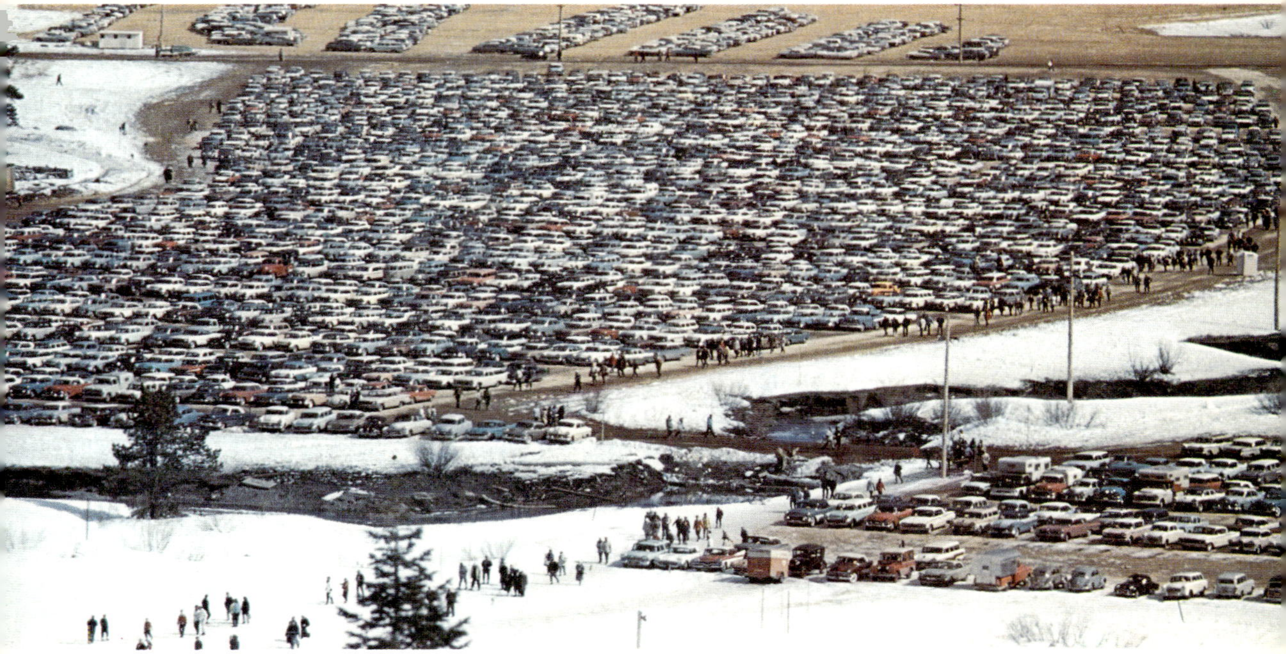

The organizers of the Olympic Games have to think of a thousand and one things . . . whether the flags of the various countries are correct . . . whether there is enough parking space available (above, the car park at Squaw Valley) . . . Only then can the first visitors be greeted. In Tokyo in 1964 this was done in a most original way (below)

heats. Zimny of Poland set the pace and Halberg stayed as back-marker for the first couple of laps. Gradually the New Zealander moved up through the field until, three laps from home, he suddenly sprinted away, creating a 30-yard gap between himself and the following bunch. By the time he reached the bell, Halberg was patently tiring, and the last lap must have been agony for him for it was very slow and he struggled all the way round. It was a tantalizing last stage because the German Grodotzki and Zimny fought every yard of it in Halberg's wake, themselves struggling but desperately trying to make up the lost ground and closing on him all the time. From somewhere or other Halberg summoned the guts to put in a final spurt that kept him just clear at the tape, after which he collapsed. The time was nearly four seconds slower than Kuts' record, but as a race it had been inspiring.

Records toppled in the 10,000 metres and in the 3,000 metres steeplechase. In the former, a slow time at the halfway stage promised a pedestrian race, but then Bolotnikov of the USSR and Dave Power of Australia took the lead, quickening the pace. Grodotzki and another Russian, Desyatchikov, were also up there with them. Bolotnikov, however, proved to be the best tactician, striking on the back straight of the penultimate lap and running a consistently fast final 400 metres which gave the others no chance of catching him. Grodotzki took the silver, as he had done in the 5,000 metres, and Power the bronze, and all three were inside Kuts' Olympic record. The latter's world record, however, still stood. In the steeplechase, the Pole, Krzyszkowiak, ran an attractive race to lop 7 seconds off Christopher Brasher's 1956 Olympics record, and the Russians picked up the other two medals.

Division of spoils

The field events were, as usual, roughly divided between the might of the United States and the might of the Soviet Union. The Americans won the shot, the discus and the long jump; the Russians won the hammer, the javelin and the high jump. In the shot putt, Parry O'Brien at last surrendered his grip on the gold and let in Bill Nieder, who had only just qualified for the US team but returned to form at the right moment and achieved a record 65 feet 6¾ inches. Al Oerter beat his own record at the discus to score his second successive Olympic victory. Tsibulenko won the javelin, and Rudenkov the hammer in a new record. The first two high jumpers were both Russian, Shavlakadze being the more consistent but the silver medalist, Brumel, seemed to have greater potential. John Thomas, the world record holder, had to be content with the bronze. The nationalities were reversed in the long jump, Boston and Roberson (USA) winning the gold and silver, the young Ter-Ovanesyan (USSR) the bronze. In the women's field events, however, the Russians had the strength and the weight, winning the long jump, the javelin, the shot and the discus, Tamara Press winning the shot with a record and collecting the silver for the discus behind Ponomaryeva. In the javelin came a name to recall the ghosts of earlier Olympics—Dana Zatopekova, wife of the great Zatopek, had of course won the javelin gold way back in 1952 in the same year as her husband's triumphs. Now, in Rome, she came again to win a silver. Finally, in the high jump, the world

A view of the enormous construction works round the Olympic Stadium in Munich

record holder, Iolanda Balas of Roumania, was so superior to everyone else that she jumped 5½ inches higher than her nearest rival. The silver was shared by Jozwiakowska of Poland and Dorothy Shirley of Great Britain, a compensation for Britain after Mary Bignal (later Mary Rand) had faltered in the long jump and failed to qualify for the last six.

American revenge

In the swimming pool, in the magnificent Stadio del Nueto America avenged the drubbing received at the hands of the Australians in 1956 by winning eleven golds to Australia's five. Australia's Murray Rose retained his 400 metres

The opening ceremonies at Olympic Games are as much a fashion parade as a show of national athletic strength

title, surprisingly beating Jon Konrads who was forced into third place by Yamanaka of Japan. Konrads, however, had his revenge over Rose in the 1,500 metres, which he won in a new Olympic record of 17 minutes 19·6 seconds. The United States won all the relays, and Australia's only success in the women's events was Dawn Fraser's win in the 100 metres freestyle, her

A model showing the principle features of Munich's "Olympic city": **1** *Olympic stadium* **2** *Main hall* **3** *Swimming pool* **4** *Small sports hall* **5** *Cycling track* **6** *Show-jumping arena* **7** *Volleyball hall* **8** *Hockey pitches* **9** *Training area* **10** *Olympic village* **11** *Radio and Television centre* **12** *Press buildings* **13** *Railway station* **14** *Underground railway station* **15** *Television tower* **16** *Artificial lake* **17** *Open-air stage* **18** *Panoramic viewing-point* **19** *Car parks* **20** *Olympic construction company*

second consecutive Olympic success. The Americans this time proved to be real mermaids of the water, breaking the world record in both relays, their star performer being Christine Von Saltza, who herself created a new Olympic best for the 400 metres freestyle. Britain won a gold in the 200 metres breaststroke in the very determined person of Anita Lonsbrough, who pursued the German Wiltrud Urselmann all the way, taking the lead only 25 metres from home and setting a new world record of 2 minutes 49·5 seconds.

The Rome Olympics, like all other Olympics, were characterized by the variety of highlights, some more incidental than others, depending upon the degree of interest they created. In the cycling events, for example, Italian national pride was given a tremendous boost as their riders totally eclipsed the French and won five of the six gold medals. In the 50 kilometres walk a diminutive Englishman named Don Thompson won a gold medal wearing a species of headgear that looked as if it had been borrowed from Beau Geste. He then waved it joyfully at the crowd as if to say that mad dogs and Englishmen may go out in the midday sun, but the Englishmen come away with the medals. In the decathlon a remarkable climax was reached when the two leading contenders, Rafer Johnson of the United States and Yang Chuan Kwang of Nationalist China (both incidentally friends at the same university in Los Angeles) were separated by only 67 points with just the 1,500 metres to run. Yang needed to win by a margin of 10 seconds to take the gold, but Johnson, staggering with fatigue, held on to stay within range, crossing the line just a few yards behind and winning the Olympic title by the very slender difference of 58 points.

Two names for the future

Lastly, two examples of how the Olympics have a habit of producing stars as if from out of a hat. Inside the ropes of the boxing ring, a young 18-year-old named Cassius Clay danced about rather showily but threw some impressively fast combination clusters of punches, winning for himself the first major accolade of his career, a gold medal. In the ancient streets of Rome, a barefoot unknown named Abebe Bikila, member of the Imperial Life Guards attached to the Royal Household of the Kingdom of Ethiopia, padded along in the darkness towards the finishing line beside the Arch of Constantine, far ahead of the rest of the field. Then the darkness gave way all round him as the lights from the motorcycles and cars, from the streetlamps, torches and the photographers' flashbulbs focused on this new hero of the greatest race of all in his moment of simple and traditional joy. He had won the Marathon.

The Olympics come to Asia—Tokyo 1964

The Tokyo Games were probably the best organized of all. To accommodate nearly 6,000 competitors, representing a new record entry of 94 countries, the Japanese spent more than 550 million dollars, and their meticulous attention to detail, together with the consideration and courtesy of their hospitality, won universal praise. War had prevented the games being held in Tokyo in 1940; now, twenty-four years later, the omission was repaired and the Olympics came to Asia for the first time.

Eight months before this, however, in the snows of late January and early February, the IXth Winter

The Olympic flame at the 1968 sailing championships in Acapulco

A plan of Kiel, the location for the sailing events in 1972. **1** *The Olympic flame* **2** *Area for the opening and closing ceremonies* **3** *Information centre for visitors, bank and exchange bureau, travel agency, lost-property office, post office* **4** *Promenade, shops* **5** *Information office* **6** *Organizational headquarters* **7** *Press centre* **8** *Salt-water swimming pool, sauna baths, massaging, first aid* **9** *Boatyard: surveying, workshop, sailmaking* **10** *Recreation centre, all-purpose hall, restaurant with terrace* **11** *Lodgings for journalists* **12** *Olympic living-quarters* **13** *Dry moorings for competitors' boats* **14** *Hotel*

Opposite: *The 1968 sailing championships in Acapulco Bay. Seen here are the gold medal winners in the Flying Dutchman class, Pattisson and McDonald-Smith of Great Britain. Their boat was called "Supercalifragilistic-expialidocious"*

Olympics had taken place in and around the ancient Tyrolean city of Innsbruck. Here too, admirable organization was apparent, for in fact the snows for once were absent, at least from the sky. It was only thanks to the foresight of the Austrians that all the events took place; somehow they managed to preserve the snow that had fallen previously and filled in the gaps on the ski courses where necessary. There was an unhappy prelude to the competitions in that the British tobogganist, Skrzypecki, and the Australian skier, Milne, were both killed while training, and a few moments' silence was observed at the opening ceremony which took place in the shadow of the awesome Bergisel ski-jump.

When the competitive events took place the chief stars to emerge were all women. In the speed skating the young blonde Russian, Lydia Skoblikova, followed up her double medal success in Squaw Valley by becoming the first person ever to win four gold medals at an Olympic meeting. She won all the four events, three of them in record time, and achieved this quadruple triumph in the space of four days. In the Alpine skiing, two cheerful French sisters, Christine and Marielle Goitschel, under twenty years of age, brought off a spectacular double. In the giant slalom, Marielle took the gold and Christine the silver; in the slalom Christine took the gold and Marielle the silver. On both occasions the bronze was won by Jean Saubert of the United States. In the third of the women's Alpine skiing events all three medals went to Austria, Christl Haas taking the gold, followed by Edith Zimmermann and Traudl Hecher.

The opening event of the Innsbruck Games certainly had star quality in the persons of its winners, Oleg Protopopov and Ludmilla Belousova, who captured the gold in the pairs figure skating and delighted not only the gallery at the rinkside but millions who watched them on television. Seldom can skill have been so supremely matched with artistic grace in a pair of skaters, and their performance was the more captivating for the way in which they radiated their pleasure in performing it. In the individual figure skating the German, Manfred Schnelldorfer, defeated Alain Calmat of France, but public attention focused, not surprisingly, on the bronze medalist, an American boy named Scott Allen who had skated to this precocious triumph at the age of 14 years 11 months. The women's figure-skating brought Holland her first gold medal for sixteen years,

The President of the Munich Olympic Committee displays outsize copies of the 1972 Olympic medal

FD
K163

and Sjoukje Dijkstra became a name for the Dutch to conjure with after the lean period since Fanny Blankers-Koen had triumphed in London.

Miscellaneously, the Russians won the ice hockey, the Germans won the tobogganing, and, surprise of the Games, the British won the two-man bobsled, the first gold medal ever to be won by Britain at a Winter Olympics and a tremendous *tour de force* by the team of Anthony Nash and Robin Dixon. This result was a surprise only in so far as the British had been greatly helped and encouraged prior to the Games by the Italians, notably by the great Eugenio Monti. Now the Italian teams were reduced to taking the silver and bronze medals by their pupils, and poor Monti was denied yet again his dream of the gold. There was one sentimental victory, however, that of the 35-year-old Swede, Sixten Jernberg, in the 50 kilometres cross-country of the Nordic skiing. He was also to win a gold in the 4 × 10 kilometres relay. In three Olympics his medal haul had been four gold, three silver, and two bronze.

A damp Summer Games

The snow did not fall at Innsbruck but the rain did at Tokyo, almost the only dampener on the Summer Olympics. Nevertheless the Japanese public loyally and interestedly packed the stadium, and perhaps their keen interest helped to spur on the competitors for, in spite of the damp conditions, an impressive number of records were broken. The rain poured down during the heats for the 100 metres, which made for leisurely times, but in fine weather in the semi-finals Bob Hayes, the American, ran superbly to record 9·9 seconds. The crowd were exultant to hear that the 10-second barrier had finally been penetrated —this was later discounted as a world record because it was ruled that Hayes had been assisted by the wind. In the final it was more or less a foregone conclusion that Hayes would destroy the field; this he duly did, but it was a pity that nobody came near enough to push him to another sub-10-seconds time. As it was, he recorded 10 seconds flat, creating a new Olympic record and equalling the world record. The 200 metres evolved into a duel between two Americans from Detroit, Carr and Drayton. In the final, Drayton took an early lead, but Carr turned on the power round the bend and shot through the tape a fifth of a second ahead of his rival and a fifth of a second inside Berruti's Olympic record.

The final of the 400 metres was composed of two Americans, two Britons, two Trinidadians, an Australian and a Pole. The two favourites were Larrabee (USA) and Mottley (Trinidad), though there was optimism in the British camp for the chances of their team captain, Robbie Brightwell, because he had beaten Mottley in a fast time in one of the semi-finals. On the day, however, Larrabee ran a clever tactical race, beginning slowly but finishing very fast, that brought him the gold medal ahead of Mottley, and Brightwell could not manage to overtake Badenski of Poland for the bronze. No records were broken, nor were any in the hurdles event over the same distance. Cawley (USA), the favourite, seemed to mistime his approach to at least two hurdles, allowing Cooper of Great Britain and Morale of Italy to take a clear lead. He recovered somehow and, with a burst of speed on the ground, stamped his superior class on the race, winning eventually by a

A poster for the Olympic Games in Tokyo, 1964

Kilius and Bäumler came to Innsbruck as favourites for the pairs title. Postcards were printed with the words "Olympic Champions 1964". But the gold medal was won by Belousova and Protopopov . . .

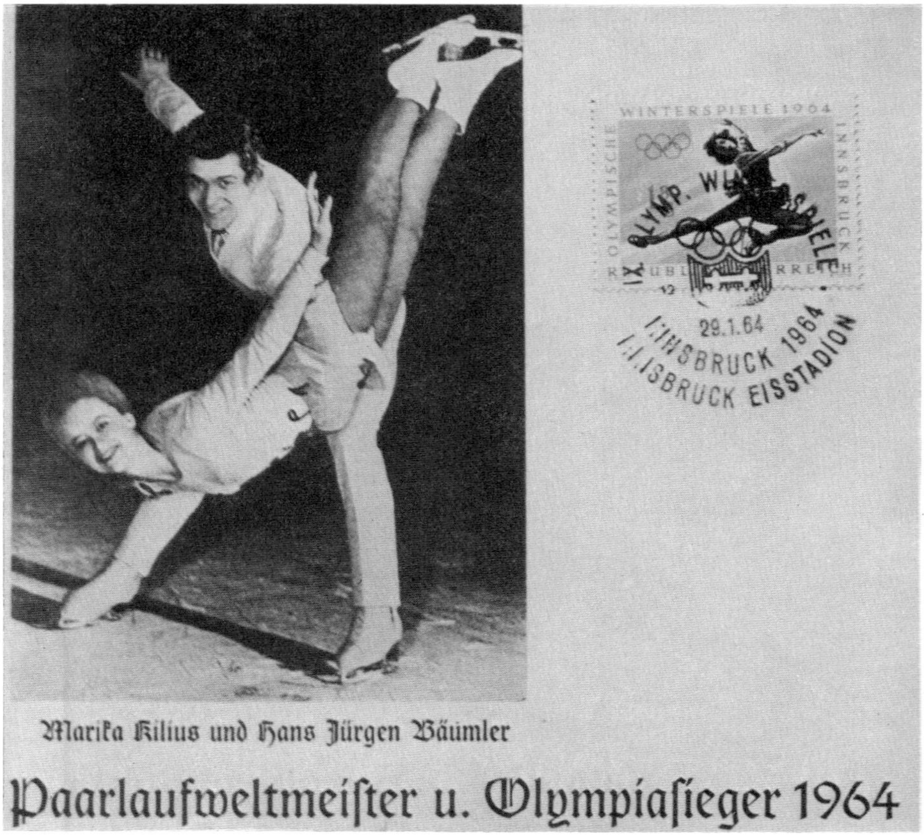

Skating judges give their verdicts

margin of half-a-second. A determined Cooper took the silver medal.

The 800 metres and the 1,500 metres belonged to Peter Snell, the man who had won the shorter event at Rome and who had been training for the longer one in Tokyo, but in the end ran both. His victories brought him the distinction of being the only middle-distance runner to have won three Olympic gold medals. In the 800 metres the heats did not come alive until Kerr of Jamaica and Kiprugut of Kenya came in first and second in one of the semi-finals and both broke Snell's Rome Olympic record. The New Zealander was probably nettled by this effrontery because he showed absolutely no mercy in the final. In spite of being badly boxed, he found enough room to squeeze past and leave the field gasping with the incredible turn of

speed which was his great hallmark. By the time he reached the tape he was cruising four yards clear of the Canadian Crothers with stamina in reserve. Kiprugut, by a gallant effort, collected the bronze for he had tripped and nearly fallen 50 metres from home when he was caught by Kerr's heel. At the line it was Kerr who was sprawling on his face, just outside the medals but, like the medalists, within the Olympic record. Snell's new time was 1 minute 45·1 seconds.

In the 1,500 metres, as in the 800 metres, it was a question of the crowd waiting for the final, and then in the final waiting for the last lap when Snell would show his

Ice hockey players on the players' bench before a match

In the most exciting game of the 1968 Olympics Czechoslovakia defeated the USSR 5–4

greatness. Unfortunately, as far as records were concerned, the other runners appeared to be waiting for Snell too and the first three laps were disappointingly slow. Snell, as usual, looked uncomfortable at such a slow pace, his style constricted and ungainly, but at 1,200 metres he caught fire, his stride lengthened, his arms pumped him forward into that magnificent surging burst of speed and he was clear of the field. The crowd roared. Coming down the home stretch, he was able to look over his shoulder for possible challengers, but there were none. He had run the last lap in 52·7 seconds. Odlozil of Czechoslovakia just beat Davies, also of New Zealand, in a scramble for the silver.

Snell's and Davies's boosts to the New Zealand medal count were more than necessary to compensate for the shock elimination of Murray Halberg, gold medallist in Rome, in the heats of the 5,000 metres. With Halberg out and Gammoudi of Tunisia unable to compete, the final had no great air of expectancy about it. Ron Clarke led for most of the race until Dellinger (USA) sprinted ahead taking the Frenchman Jazy and Norpoth of Germany with him. It looked an absolute certainty for Jazy until he unexpectedly faded in the back straight, and Bob Schul of the United States appeared from nowhere to beat Norpoth and Dellinger, in that order, to the line. The time was a slow 13 minutes 48·8 seconds.

The 10,000 metres proved to be a much more exciting race, and here again Clarke hammered out the pace from the front. As the laps went by, the challengers dropped away like flies, and they included among their number Lindgren, the US champion and record holder. It became apparent that the race was going to be decided between Clarke, Gammoudi, Wolde of Ethiopia and Billy Mills, the American Indian Marine. The efforts of these four were complicated by the fact that they were lapping sizeable groups of runners and had to sprint past them to avoid being baulked. Mills probably suffered worst of all on this score. By the time they reached the bell, Wolde had faded, and Clarke and Mills were struggling for the lead. In a dramatic last lap, Gammoudi stole up on them and sprinted past down the back straight, looking a clear winner as he opened up a 10-yard gap. But then Clarke, in mounting excitement, was seen to be gradually closing on Gammoudi as they rounded the final bend. As all eyes watched the tremendous duel between the Tunisian and the Australian, Mills put in a remarkable finishing sprint that carried him up to these two, and then past them as he sustained the burst all the way to the tape. Gammoudi held off Clarke for the

An outward appearance of confidence is perhaps the best way to overcome inner tension—the victorious Canadian four man bob team before the start in Innsbruck, 1964

Opposite: *Even in such hard-fought sports as judo and boxing, there is supposed to be fair play*

The winners get the limelight, the losers have the consolation of having at least taken part in the Games; but it is sometimes hard to conceal disappointment after years of hard training

silver, but all three broke Bolotnikov's Olympic record. Mills won in 28 minutes 24·4 seconds. It was a truly momentous finish, and rare indeed in a race of this length to see the first three crossing the line within the space of one and a half seconds.

Two golds for Britain

If New Zealand had cause to rejoice in the middle-distance running, Britain had reason to do so in the long jump. In the men's event the Welshman, Lynn Davies, who only managed to qualify for the final with his last jump, plucked the gold medal out of the air with a leap of 26 feet $5\frac{3}{4}$ inches. On a day of gusty wind and rain, he had chosen a moment of fortuitous calm to make his British record-breaking jump.

Success in the women's event brought Britain her first athletics gold in the history of the women's Olympics and it was won, fittingly, by one of the most gifted athletes of the Games—Mary Rand—who, in addition, captured a silver in the pentathlon and a bronze in the 400 metres relay race. In the long jump, she led from start to finish, broke the 1964 Olympics record on every single jump and finally soared past the world record to achieve

A water-polo match in Mexico City

22 feet 2¼ inches. It made up in good measure for the disappointments of Rome.

The same could not be said for John Thomas, the American high jumper. Favourite for the 1960 gold, he had been forced by the Russians Shavlakadze and Brumel to settle for the bronze; now once more he was beaten by Brumel, though both cleared the same height (7 ft 1¾ in.), Brumel winning on fewer failures. Dallas Long of the USA won the shot, and Al Oerter completed a splendid hat-trick of golds in the discus by out-throwing his own Olympic record by almost 4 feet. In the women's throwing events, the redoubtable Tamara Press walked off with the shot and the discus titles, and a promising 17-year-old Roumanian called Michaela Penes won the javelin with startling ease. In the walking events, Britain won a 20 kilometres gold (Ken Matthews) and a 50 kilometres silver (Paul Nihill), the latter being the loser of a tremendous tussle with Abdon Pamich of Italy. Britain also won a silver in the 3,000 metres steeplechase in the person of Maurice Herriott, but he was not really within challenging distance of the resourceful Gaston Roelants, who apparently raced after being given a pain-killing injection for an injury and hurdled beautifully throughout.

The United States seemed to have produced another Rudolph as Wyomia Tyus, also of Tennessee, flowed away from the field in the 100 metres, beating the favourite, her team-mate McGuire (who in fact won the 200 metres in a new Olympic record of 23·0 seconds). In a new feature of the women's track events, the 400 metres, Betty Cuthbert brought her haul of Olympic gold medals up to four, beating Ann Packer (Great Britain) by a fifth of a second. It was a pity that political reasons had barred the North Korean world record holder Shin Kim Dan from taking part and settling the doubts of those who questioned the authenticity of her world record times. Shin Kim Dan supposedly held the 800 metres world record (unofficially), so her presence might have made for a fine duel between her and Ann Packer. As it was, the British girl won extremely convincingly and set an official new world and Olympic record of 2 minutes 1·1 seconds.

In the swimming events, the superstar was undoubtedly Don Schollander of the United States, who at 18 years of age won four gold medals, was disappointed at not getting a fifth and showed himself capable of producing an acceleration in the water that has probably never been surpassed. It was partly thanks to Schollander of course that the United States once more bestrode the swimming events like a Colossus; in the individual events they won eight gold medals, eight silver and eight bronze, and they won all five relays, each of them in a new world record time. Australia nevertheless had a heroine of the pool. In the spring of that year Dawn Fraser had been compelled to spend several weeks in a plaster cast following a car accident, which had also tragically involved the death of her mother. In addition she was 27 years old, and most swimmers have reached their peak well before then. Yet after the 100 metres freestyle she was standing on the top of the victory rostrum for the third successive Olympics, in itself a unique hat-trick, and not only that, she had broken the one-minute barrier with a time of 59·5.

The remarkable Bikila

There was another outstanding

Sawo Kato on the rings. He won two individual golds in 1968

victor in Tokyo who likewise scorned recent physical discomfiture in climbing back to the top. Abebe Bikila had come trotting through the streets of Rome in 1960 unknown and unexpected. In 1964 he came to Tokyo an acknowledged Marathon champion, but scarcely a favourite to win it again on account of the fact that only five weeks previously he had had his appendix removed. Yet without fuss, and apparently without the excessive expenditure of effort which so frequently tortures the participants in this race, he won by more than four minutes, establishing a world record in the process and afterwards limbering up by the track as though he had been on a gentle Sunday afternoon jog. He had broken an exceptionally strong field which included Basil Heatley of Britain (who came second), Ron Clarke (who came ninth), and Jim Hogan of Eire who shared the lead with Bikila until the 35 kilometre mark. No man had won the Marathon twice; now Bikila had done it, after an operation, with such ease at the age of 32 there seemed every likelihood that he would repeat the performance at the next Olympics. At least for the hospitable Japanese there was the excitement of seeing their own man, Tsuburaya, running round the stadium for a medal and only a last desperate sprint by Heatley changed its colour from silver to bronze.

Lastly, as so often in the Olympic boxing events, particularly the heavier divisions, there was the opportunity to gaze into a crystal ball and wonder whether fame or fortune would catch up with any of the winners. In Tokyo the heavyweight gold was won by a 20-year-old black American, who was described by one reporter on the spot as having "a superb left hook, but alas, little else". The boxer was Joe Frazier.

Four great athletes from the USA—the victorious 1600 metres relay team at Tokyo

Ron Clarke, world record holder and one of the greatest distance runners of all time, was strangely dogged by bad luck at the Olympic Games

Altitude and politics— Mexico 1968

And so to the XIXth Games, the most controversial in the history of the modern Olympics. It seemed, before they started, that everything was conspiring to make these Games the very contradiction of the principles in which they were first envisaged by Baron Pierre de Coubertin. "There will be those that will die," warned a respected athletics coach when it was announced that Mexico City, over 7,000 feet above sea-level, had been selected, and all across the world, but especially in those countries at or around sea-level, similar fears were expressed about the effects of the altitude. The spectacle which people formed in their minds of distance runners staggering round the track, clawing the air and gasping for breath like marooned fish, certainly seemed a far cry from the Olympic ideal which aspired to gather the athletic best of the world to take part in fair, honourable and friendly competition. As a result, there was strong pressure to force the International Olympic Committee to

Abebe Bikila, twice winner of the Olympic Marathon, was later dealt a cruel blow by fate—he was almost completely paralyzed in a car accident

Livio Berutti, winner of the 200 metres in 1960, was not only an elegant young man, but also delighted the spectators with the easy grace of his running

change the venue from Mexico to somewhere where all nations could compete on an equal basis, and where lives, or at any rate health, would not be endangered. But the Committee remained unmoved by argument.

In the event, nobody did die. At least, not in the stadium. Shortly before the Olympics opened, a demonstration of some 5,000 people in the Plaza of the Three Cultures in Mexico City ended in bloodshed, with a great number (it has never been revealed exactly how many) shot dead by the army and the secret police. The demonstration had been brutally suppressed so that the Olympic Games could proceed without fear of political interruption. However, it did not escape the notice of many people in the watching world, that while millions of dollars had been spent on preparations for the Games, no amount of money could envelop Mexico City in an atmosphere that was fair to all competitors.

Nobody died in the Olympic stadium, but the effects of the altitude were plain to see and they are preserved in the record books. World and Olympic records fell like ninepins but it is significant that, on the track, they only fell in the short events. It was predicted that for the "explosive" events—sprinting, jumping, throwing—the records would topple because the thinness of the air offered less resistance; equally, it was predicted that the "endurance" events—the longer track races—would be slower, and so it proved. Times for the 3,000 metres steeplechase and upwards were, by Olympic standards, distinctly slow and the medal-winners for these races were mostly people who were born and bred in countries of high altitude, or who had spent months training in the hills. Some

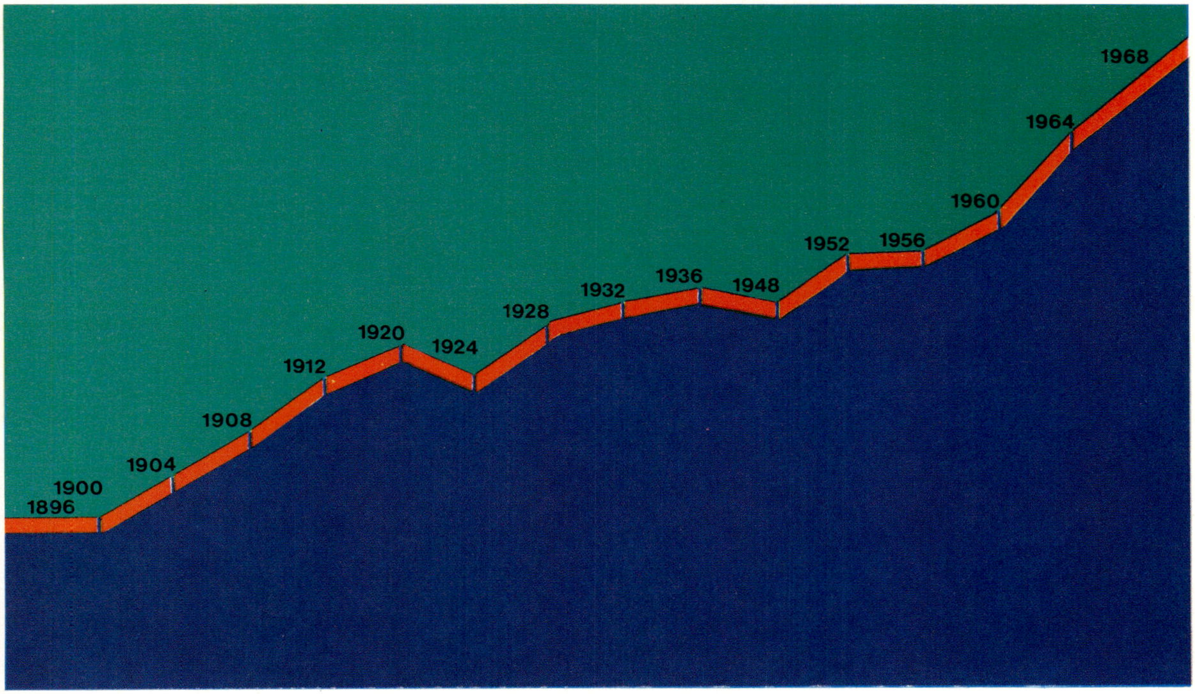

Chart showing the improvement in performance in the pole-vault:

1896: **10′10″**	*1900:* **10′10″**	*1904:* **11′6″**	*1908:* **12′2″**
1912: **12′11½″**	*1920:* **13′5″**	*1924:* **12′11½″**	*1928:* **13′9¼″**
1932: **14′1⅞″**	*1936:* **14′3¼″**	*1948:* **14′1¼″**	*1952:* **14′11¼″**
1956: **14′11½″**	*1960:* **15′5″**	*1964:* **16′8¾″**	*1968:* **17′8½″**

of them were also people who had been decisively beaten in races at sea-level by runners who were now struggling far down the finishing order, and this factor was to many the crowning injustice of what they called "The Unfair Games."

As if the problems of altitude and politics were not enough, the Olympic vision was now blurred by the spectre of commercialism. This had blown up at the time of the Winter Olympics which had been held in February in and around Grenoble, France. The I.O.C. had tried to curb advertising and commercial exploitation by banning trade names from appearing on skis. Unfortunately most of the leading skiers had been given their equipment by the manufacturers and been financially assisted by them in other ways, in the manufacturers' obvious hope of gaining valuable advertising rewards from the skiers' success. Skiing is an expensive sport and few of the top names would be able to practise it seriously without this help from the ski-equipment companies. So the disqualification of trade names by the I.O.C. was not greeted with enthusiasm. Eventually a compromise was reached; the trade names could remain on the skis, but the skiers should not be photographed or televised with them. As a compromise this was successful enough, but it failed to solve any

Opposite: *Randy Matson, winner of the 1968 Olympic shot putt with a distance of 67 feet 4¾ inches*

long-term problems as regards the distinction between amateurism and professionalism, and the Summer Olympics in Mexico were still to be tarnished by stories of athletes being bribed by sportswear manufactuers.

Killy, hero of France

When the Winter Olympics got under way, having been launched with great pomp by President de Gaulle, they belonged appropriately enough to a Frenchman—Jean-Claude Killy—who became only the second man to win three Alpine gold medals in a Games. Killy won the downhill in a time of 1 minute 59·85 seconds, eight-hundredths of a second faster than his team-mate Guy Perillat, whose time had seemed invincible when he had been the only one of the first batch of skiers to break 2 minutes. In the end, Killy and Perillat were the only competitors to do so. Killy then won the giant slalom by a margin of more than 2 seconds from Willy Favre of Switzerland, and completed his triple gold triumph by taking the slalom, though this event was marred by controversy. The race took place in dreadful weather conditions, with visibility in places down to only

Grace, poise and impeccable style brought Peggy Fleming the figure skating gold in Grenoble

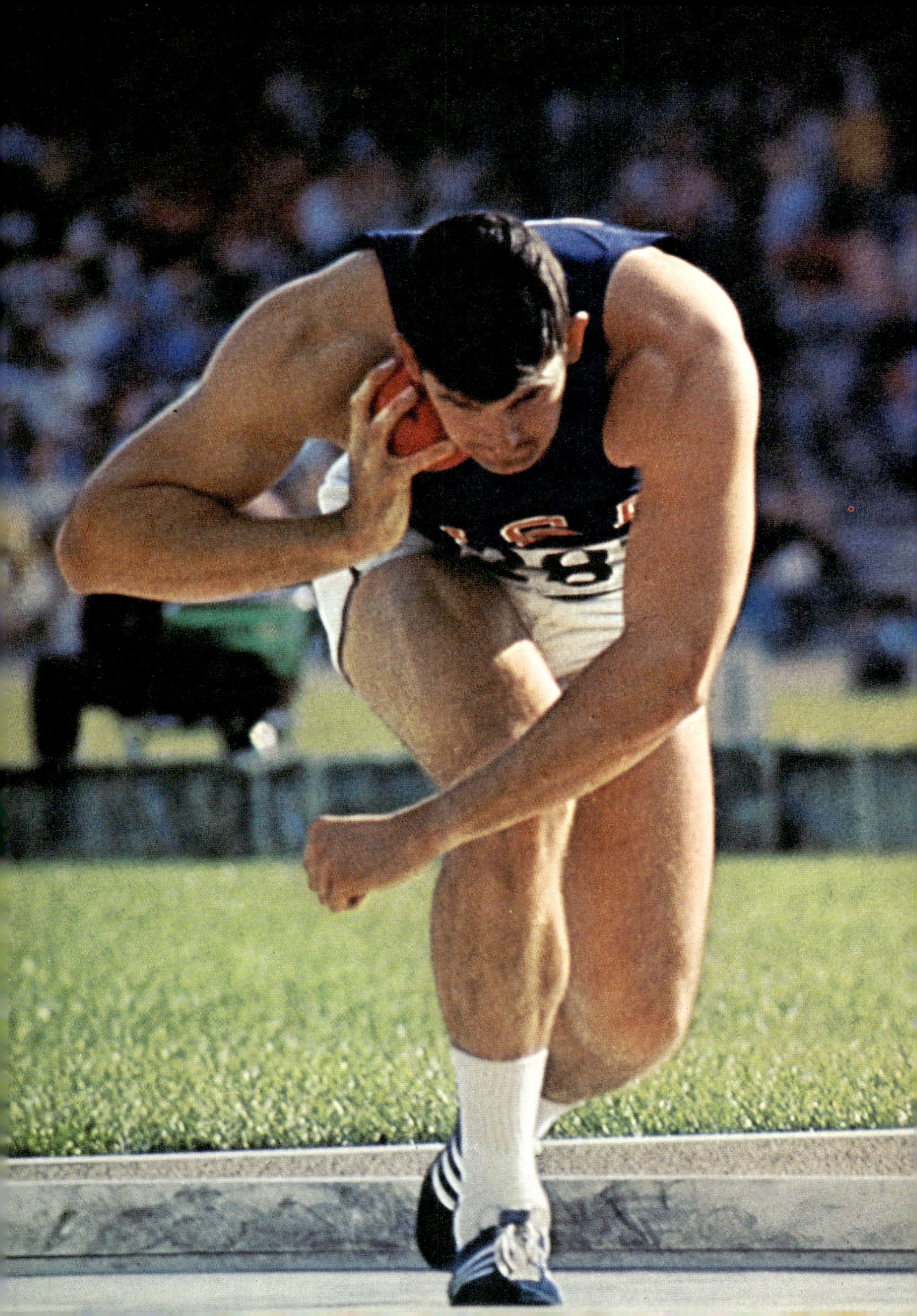

Al Oerter, four times winner of the Olympic discus title

a few yards. Time and again the skiers were delayed until a gap appeared in the mist. Killy recorded fast times but these were overtaken by Mjoen of Norway, and then by Karl Schranz of Austria. Mjoen was immediately disqualified for missing two gates; Schranz however had been given a re-run after claiming that an interloper had forced him to pull up by crossing his path in the first run. This claim was later dismissed by the judges, Schranz disqualified, and so Killy won in less happy circumstances than he must have wished. Nevertheless, his overall superiority, his great ability to attack all the way, were unquestioned in these Games, and he became the idol of all France.

In the women's events the French had less success than they might have hoped, though Marielle Goitschel, one of the two famous sisters who had won such honours at Innsbruck in 1964, took the gold medal in the slalom ahead of the Canadian Nancy Greene, and France also had the bronze medal-winner, Annie Famose. In this race Britain missed a medal by a fraction, Gina Hathorn taking fourth place, only three-hundredths of a second behind Famose. For the first time in the history of the Winter Olympics, British competitors had come into the reckoning in the skiing, and their three hopes all did well—Bunny Field came sixth in the downhill and Divina Galica came eighth in the giant slalom. Nancy Greene might have been Queen of the Games had there not been problems with the weather, which changed abruptly during the course of the downhill race. And both she and Divina Galica were hampered because their skis had been wrongly waxed and missed the chance of a medal. In this race Austria captured the gold and the bronze in the persons of Olga Pall and Christl Haas respectively, and Isabelle Mir (France) won the silver. Greene, however, stamped her class on the giant slalom, winning by the astonishing margin of more than 2·5 seconds.

Yamashita Matsuda performing a one-armed hand-stand on the bar

Boris Schaklin of the USSR on the pommel-horse

Monti wins at last

Probably the most sentimental triumph of the Winter Games was that of Eugenio Monti, the Italian veteran of the bobsleigh. Forty years old, he had won the world two-man bob title seven times, the world four-man title twice, but never an Olympics. Now at Alpe d'Huez, on a problem track which had to be artificially frozen on some of the corners because of the sun's heat

during the day, Monti dramatically came out with the gold in both the two-man and four-man events. Another vastly popular victory belonged to a pair of skaters who were also comparative veterans—the Protopopovs of Russia, gold medal winners in 1964, world champions in 1963 and 1966, and now surely competing for the last time in the Winter Olympics. With their unique blend of grace and skill, they delighted the crowd and, with an almost flawless performance, took the gold ahead of their great rivals from Moscow, Tatyana Joukchesternava and Alex Gorelik. America's Peggy Fleming won the women's figure skating with an exhibition of great technical expertise, and Wolfgang Schwarz (Austria) captured the men's gold ahead of Wood of America and Pera of France. Schwarz's great rival and compatriot, Emmerich Danzer, finished in fourth place. Finally, the Russians won the gold medal in the ice hockey, the Czechs the silver, but the highlight of this particular competition was the match between these two countries which the Czechs won 5–4. It was the Russians' only defeat and was dispassionately applauded. By the time of the Summer Olympics political developments would mean that any Czech victory over Russia would receive a more emotional response.

Mexico had other politics too, both before the Games with the exclusion of South Africa and the riots in the city, and during them when Tommie Smith and John Carlos made their famous Black Power demonstration on the victory rostrum. The two American sprinters had given signal of their intentions by running in black socks in both the heats and the final, and when they came out for the medal ceremony they wore in addition a black glove on one hand. As their National Anthem was played they raised the gloved hand in a clenched fist salute and bowed their heads. For the officials of the United States team this performance came as a shock, but to the world at large, who saw it on television and pictured in the newspapers, it was a gesture that grew in stature as people understood it. Smith and Carlos were making the plain statement that they would only be accepted as first-class citizens in their own country because they were Olympic champions. They had attained a most public place for their demonstration by their ability to run fast.

In the 200 metres nobody in fact could run as fast as Smith; coming off the bend he really slipped into top gear and, in an astonishing burst of speed, left the field trailing to record a new world and Olympic record of 19·8 seconds. Carlos, who was expected to be his closest rival, was surprisingly beaten into third place by Peter Norman of Australia. Smith's running was the second superstar performance in the sprints. In the 100 metres Jim Hines had earned himself the accolade of "fastest man on earth" when he had raced ahead of his rivals to breast the tape in 9·9 seconds, breaking the magical barrier of 10 seconds to create a new Olympic record and equal the world record which he and Charlie Greene had unofficially set up in California earlier in 1968. Here in Mexico, Charlie Greene was edged out of the silver by Lennox Miller of Jamaica, but both were given a time of 10·0 seconds. It was the first all-black final in the history of the Olympics. Charlie Greene, one of the characters of the Games, ran in dark glasses which he apparently called his "re-entry peepers", worn to prevent him being blinded by his own speed!

Jumping every jump: Marion Coakes, winner of the show-jumping silver medal in 1968

Tokyo, 1964: Yuri Vlasov, until this moment the world's strongest man, is finally beaten in the weightlifting

Yet another world record was toppled in the 400 metres, and the first three home—Evans, James and Freeman (all USA)—all broke the Olympic record of 44·9 seconds. Evans recorded the astonishing time of 43·8 with James just one-tenth of a second behind him. These three men, together with Vince Matthews, later won the 1,600 metres relay race with an almost inevitable ease, reducing the world record by 3·5 seconds to the extraordinary time of 2 minutes 56·1 seconds, which means an average of 44 seconds per man. This gives some indication of the incredible strength of the United States' sprinters, and shows too the effects of the TARTAN track and the altitude, which helped the winners to achieve record-breaking times in all the sprint events.

Not so in the distance races. On the first day of the athletics, the 10,000 metres was run and immediately the Games had a sacrificial victim. His name was Ron Clarke, current holder of the world record for this event and for the 5,000 metres, a man who had inexplicably never won an Olympic gold. With the best of his running days almost gone, it seemed certain that he had to win in Mexico or never. For this he had trained and trained, but probably he knew that

Tokyo 1964: a new Hercules emerges victorious—Leonid Zhabotinsky wins the gold medal

in this oxygen-starved atmosphere the odds against him outlasting the runners from the altitude countries were long. Early on, the pace was slow and the field of 37 stayed bunched. A record was out of the question. By the time they had run 4,000 metres the leading group had been cut to 15 runners, and one man (Santos of Honduras) had been carried away on a stretcher. With four laps to go the pace quickened, and only seven men were in contention, led by Mamo Wolde of Ethiopia who had come fourth in this event in 1964. The other six were Clarke of Australia, Temu and Keino of Kenya, Gammoudi of Tunisia, Sviridov of Russia, and the much-cheered local boy, Martinez of Mexico. With three laps to go, at the point where Clarke would normally have made his move and outstripped the field, it was obvious he could not find the response in his limbs, and Wolde continued to lead. Clarke gradually slipped back, Keino collapsed on the grass (throughout the Games he was suffering from gallstones), and the race became a struggle between Temu and Wolde. Wolde accelerated but Temu hung on, and then in a truly magnificent finishing burst raced past the Ethiopian to win in a canter, though his time of 29 minutes 27·4 seconds was

Not all events take place in front of huge crowds . . . for some competitors the only spectators are the judges

almost two minutes slower than Clarke's world record. Gammoudi picked up the bronze, and Martinez and Sviridov beat poor Clarke into sixth place, followed by Ron Hill of Britain. One yard over the finishing line, Clarke collapsed and oxygen was administered to him, as it was to several others. Twenty minutes passed before he could even get up on his feet to be helped from the stadium. It was a sad sight, not easily forgotten by the many who cherished the hope that this great runner would be rewarded with a gold, and most of them knew that of the five men who beat him, three lived at altitude and the other two had trained for months in the mountains.

The 5,000 metres followed a similar pattern, and confirmed the

Exciting events such as ski-jumping always attract vast crowds. Above: *spectators at the Winter Olympics at Squaw Valley*

Below: *Collecting the autographs of famous athletes is sometimes taken to extraordinary lengths*

Dagmar Rom and Andrea Lawrence-Mead at the Winter Olympics in 1952, and Olga Pall (opposite) *sixteen years later. It is not only the clothes that have changed over the years: the skiing style has altered too*

Mexico City is more than 7,000 feet above sea level. The athletes had to acclimatize themselves to this unaccustomed height. This picture shows the British runner Bruce Tulloh training with "Mexican air"

prominence of the African distance and middle-distance runners in these Olympics. There were no less than six from that continent in the final, and as in the 10,000 metres they accounted for all three medals. Clarke made a brave effort to set the pace and hold the lead, but again the altitude beat him and in the end it was between Gammoudi, Keino and Temu. On the last lap it seemed almost a certainty that the two Kenyans would overtake the Tunisian, but Gammoudi had run a superbly judged tactical race and he held them off. Keino took the silver and Temu the bronze, while Martinez of Mexico came in fourth, just ahead of Clarke. The time was slow.

Kenya ascendant

Kenya was also represented in the medal-winners in the 800 metres, in the 1,500 metres, and in the steeple-

chase, a triumphant Olympics for a young country. In the 800 metres Wilson Kiprugut took the silver medal behind Ralph Doubell of Australia, both men running faster than they had ever done before, and Doubell in the process beating the Olympic record and equalling Peter Snell's world record of 1 minute 44·3 seconds. Kipchoge Keino ran a magnificent 1,500 metres final to outwit, outpace and outrun the world record holder, Jim Ryun of the USA, and break Herb Elliott's eight-year-old Olympic record by seven-tenths of a second. Behind Ryun, Bodo Tümmler of West Germany collected the bronze. In the steeplechase, Kenya won both the gold and the silver, the former going to the astounding Amos Biwott, who had never run a steeplechase until three months before the Olympics and who adopted a revolutionary method of taking the water-jumps—without getting his feet wet! In the final he came from behind in the closing stages to overtake his compatriot Kogo. Here again the altitude claimed its victims, among them Maurice Herriott of Great Britain, silver medalist in Tokyo, and now carried from the stadium on a stretcher with the familiar oxygen apparatus, having failed to qualify in the first heat.

The phenomena of Mexico

Altogether some amazing sights were seen in Mexico. In addition to Biwott's steeplechase water-jumps, a new phenomenon presented itself in the shape of the Fosbury Flop. In the high jump an American gentleman named Dick Fosbury defied convention, the coaching manuals, and apparently gravity, by clearing 7 feet $4\frac{1}{4}$ inches not only head first but backwards as well. Before the

days of foam-rubber pits he had risked serious injury with this method of jumping; now his courage and persistence had been rewarded with a gold. Earlier, in the long jump, another American gentleman named Bob Beamon had astonished the world, not to mention his fellow competitors, by clearing 29 feet 2½ inches on his first jump, putting an end there and then to competition for the gold. This quite extraordinary leap broke the previous world record by almost 2 feet. As several people remarked at the time, he had missed out the 28 feet mark altogether, going straight from 27 to 29. The other competitors, including former gold medallists Ralph Boston (1960) and Lynn Davies (1964) could only stand and rub their eyes. As for the triple jump, the previous world record was beaten by no less than five people, a somewhat disheartening statistic for those in fourth and fifth place who failed to pick up a medal.

There was one more virtuoso performance in the field events—Al Oerter from the USA became the first man to win four successive gold medals, and he did this by throwing the discus further than he had ever thrown it before. In Melbourne in 1956 he had won with a record throw of 184 feet 11 inches; by the time he stood on the victor's rostrum in Mexico twelve years later he had raised this distance to 212 feet 6½ inches, another Olympic record. This was an unexpected triumph for the United States after the disappointing showing of Jay Silvester who, earlier in the year, had thrown a new world record of 224 feet 5 inches, and here in Mexico could not manage more than a paltry 202 feet 8 inches.

A similar, slightly unexpected, triumph came the way of Great Britain in the 400 metres hurdles, though here the surprise was not so much in the victory but in the margin of victory. In the final, against formidable opposition from the USA in the person of Whitney and Vanderstock, both of whom prior to the Games had run faster times than him, David Hemery set off at an explosive pace and virtually had the race won by the time he cleared the first hurdle. Leading from beginning to end and never letting up, he gave the others no chance to close on him, and came home seven yards and nine-tenths of a second ahead of Hennige of West Germany in the amazing time of 48·1 seconds. As if a gold medal and a world record were not enough, Britain also picked up the bronze, John Sherwood running the race of his life to beat the Americans and secure for his country only the second double medal success since 1924.

Triumph and tragedy

In the women's events there was the usual blend of triumph and tragedy. Triumph was positively there for Wyomia Tyus from Tennessee, who became the first athlete of either sex successfully to defend an Olympic sprint title when she won the 100 metres in a new world record of 11·0 seconds. For Vera Nikolic there was tragedy. Strongly tipped as favourite for the 800 metres gold, she dropped out of the semi-final after only 300 metres, walked out of the stadium and, it is said, attempted to commit suicide by trying to jump from a bridge. She was caught in time, given sedation, and sent home to Yugoslavia. Many observers felt that her coach had trained her too hard, forcing her body beyond a limit that it could stand. The 800 metres was in the end won by Madeline Manning of

The closing ceremony in Mexico City

Above: *At the closing ceremony in Rome, thousands of spectators spontaneously set light to their programmes—a unique and moving firework display.* Below: *Yoshinari Sakai, who was born on the day the atomic bomb fell on Hiroshima, lit the Olympic flame in Tokyo*
Right: *Farewells are bade in Mexico City and already, in the sky, the Munich Games are anticipated*

the United States in a new Olympic record of 2 minutes 0·9 seconds. It was a pity for Britain that Lillian Board did not run in this race instead of the 200 metres where she could manage no higher than sixth place in a semi-final. She might well have challenged for the 800 metres gold, which would have been a consolation for her after her evident disappointment at being beaten to the line in the 400 metres by the surprising speed of Colette Besson of France. Lillian Board had won a silver medal at the age of nineteen, and had run her fastest-ever 400 metres, but the pressures that the press had placed on her by making her so strong a favourite for the race undoubtedly affected her and made her feel that she had failed when in fact she had been marvellously successful. Her tragically premature death has robbed the athletics world of one of its most attractive and brilliant competitors.

Overall, the Mexico Olympics were splendidly organized, and what energed from them when all the arguments about altitude had died, was that America still had a stranglehold on the sprints and on the swimming (in the latter they won 73 out of a possible 104 medals), Europe continued to dominate in cycling and the modern pentathlon, and Africa had emerged as a continent to be reckoned with in the middle and long-distance track events. This last factor was fully rubbed in as the crowd waited in the Estadio Olimpico for the leader of the Marathon to appear. Many were probably expecting the familiar figure of Abebe Bikila to come padding into the stadium on the way to his third successive gold, but he had dropped out, injured, after 17 kilometres. Instead his fellow Ethiopian Mamo Wolde loped down the ramp and onto the track, winning by a margin of more than 3 minutes from Kimihara of Japan and Ryan of New Zealand. Incredibly, he had the energy to jog round on a lap of honour, and there was not a drop of sweat to be seen on him. It was in the great tradition of Bikila.

But perhaps even this mirage fades beside the memory of Vera Caslavska, the beautiful Czech gymnast, who won four gold medals to add to the three she had won in 1964, and captured the hearts of a world-wide audience as she performed on horse, floor, beam and bars with incredible grace and agility. She had also won the heart of Josef Odlozil, silver medallist in Tokyo for the 1,500 metres, eighth here in Mexico, who became her husband in the Roman Catholic Cathedral of Xocalo Square, Mexico City, on the last day of the XIXth Olympics. It made a dream-like end to the Olympics for at least two of the participants.

Kiel
1972

München
1972

SAPPORO'72
XI Olympic Winter Gam

THE OLYMPIC GAMES 1972 SAPPORO AND MUNICH

For the Olympic Games 1972 was a year of crisis. At Sapporo, Karl Schranz, the Austrian skier, was disqualified from participating in the Games because he earned money from his sport. In the controversy that ensued, Avery Brundage stood his ground. Perhaps only he knows why Schranz was chosen as the scapegoat from the fifty or so well-paid skiers taking part.

The old problem of professionalism had reappeared. Now the International Olympic Committee, the organizing power behind the Games, must decide what can be done to restore honesty as an integral part of the Games. In the face of the growing power of commerce and national prestige, perhaps the time has come to welcome professionals in a bid to restore the element of individual striving.

At Munich, there was general admiration for the physical layout of the Games. At first, the day-to-day running of the Games functioned very smoothly. There were great sporting achievements, with new Olympic and world records being attained almost every day. Mark Spitz's seven gold medals marked a glittering record. Only in the long jump were there no sensations. The experts say Bob Beamon has monopolized this event for the future, with his 8·90 metre (29 ft. 2½ in.) jump in Mexico City.

But gradually the Games became dominated by political issues. Before they had even begun, the refusal to allow Rhodesia to take part was roundly denounced by Avery Brundage, President of the I.O.C., as a political act, completely outside the context of the Games. But soon after the start of the Games, a blatantly political and savage act resulted in the deaths of nine Israeli athletes, kidnapped from the Olympic village. No longer could politics be discounted as a force, albeit an unwelcome one, in international sport.

In 1972, Avery Brundage retired as President of the I.O.C. He has steered the Olympic Games for so long that the course which his successor, Lord Killanin, chooses to take will be watched with interest around the world. But never again perhaps will the impression of one man's personality be so firmly stamped on the Games.

Issues, suppressed for many years, were finally brought to light at Sapporo and Munich. Can Lord Killanin and his committee deal with these successfully, bearing in mind the aim of the Games: the participation by athletes of many nations in "the true spirit of sportsmanship, for the glory of sport and for the honour of our teams". The 1976 Games in Montreal and Colorado will be the test.

The torchbearer climbs the final flight of steps to set alight the Olympic flame, marking the opening of the XXth summer Olympic Games, in Munich 1972

THE WINTER OLYMPIC GAMES IN SAPPORO

ALPINE SKIING (MEN)

Downhill

1. Russi (Switzerland)
2. Collombin (Switzerland)
3. Messner (Austria)

Giant slalom

1. G. Thoeni (Italy)
2. Bruggmann (Switzerland)
3. Mattle (Switzerland)

Slalom

1. Fernandez-Ochoa (Spain)
2. G. Thoeni (Italy)
3. R. Thoeni (Italy)

Alpine combined	Points
1. G. Thoeni (Italy)	21·11
2. Tresch (Switzerland)	46·98
3. Hunter (Canada)	86·41

ALPINE SKIING (WOMEN)

Downhill

1. Nadig (Switzerland)
2. Proell (Austria)
3. Corrock (USA)

Giant slalom

1. Nadig (Switzerland)
2. Proell (Austria)
3. Drezel (Austria)

Slalom

1. Cochran (USA)
2. Debernard (France)
3. Steurer (France)

Alpine combined	Points
1. Proell (Austria)	25·64
2. Steurer (France)	59·51
3. Foerland (Norway)	80·95

NORDIC SKIING (MEN)

15 km cross-country	Minutes
1. Lundback (Sweden)	45:28·2
2. Simaschov (USSR)	46:00·8
3. Formo (Norway)	46:02·6

30 km cross-country	Hours
1. Vedenin (USSR)	1:36:31·1
2. Tyldum (Norway)	1:37:25·3
3. Harviken (Norway)	1:37:32·4

50 km cross-country	
1. Tyldum (Norway)	2:43:14·7
2. Myrmo (Norway)	2:43:29·4
3. Vedenin (USSR)	2:44:00·1

4×10 (40) km Relay	
1. USSR	2:04:47·9
2. Norway	2:04:57·0
3. Switzerland	2:07:00·0

Nordic combined (cross-country and jumping)	Points
1. Wehling (East Germany)	413·340
2. Miettinen (Finland)	405·505
3. Luck (East Germany)	398·800

Ski jumping (small hill)		
1. Kasaya (Japan)	84 + 79 m	244·2
2. Konno (Japan)	82·5 + 79 m	234·8
3. Aochi (Japan)	83·5 + 77·5 m	229·5

The experts were confounded when a complete outsider—Francisco Fernandez-Ochoa of Spain—won the gold medal in the ski slalom

Examples of the "snow sculpture" which was such a feature at Sapporo

Ski jumping (big hill)

1. Fortuna (Poland)	111 + 87·5	m	219·9
2. Steiner (Switzerland)	94 +103	m	219·8
3. Schmidt (East Germany)	98·5+101	m	219·3

Biathlon	Hours
1. Solberg (Norway)	1:15:55·5
2. Knauthe (East Germany)	1:16:07·6
3. Arwidson (Sweden)	1:16:27·0

Biathlon relay

1. USSR	1:51:44·9
2. Finland	1:54:37·2
3. East Germany	1:54:57·6

NORDIC SKIING (WOMEN)

5 km cross-country	Minutes
1. Kulakova (USSR)	17:00·5
2. Kajosmaa (Finland)	17:05·5
3. Sikolova (Czechoslovakia)	17:07·3

10 km cross-country

1. Kulakova (USSR)	34:17·8
2. Olunina (USSR)	34:54·1
3. Kajosmaa (Finland)	34:58·4

3×5 (15) km Relay

1. USSR	48:46·1
2. Finland	49:19·3
3. Norway	49:51·4

SPEED SKATING (MEN)

500 m	Seconds
1. Keller (West Germany)	39·4
2. Borjes (Sweden)	39·6
3. Muratov (USSR)	39·8

1500 m	Minutes
1. Schenk (Holland)	2:02·9
2. Gronvold (Norway)	2:04·2
3. Claesson (Sweden)	2:05·8

5000 m

1. Schenk (Holland)	7:23·6
2. Gronvold (Norway)	7:28·1
3. Stensen (Norway)	7:33·3

10,000 m

1. Schenk (Holland)	15:01·3
2. Verkerk (Holland)	15:04·7
3. Stensen (Norway)	15:07·0

SPEED SKATING (WOMEN)

500 m	Seconds
1. Henning (USA)	43·3
2. Krasnova (USSR)	44·0
3. Titova (USSR)	44·4

1000 m	Minutes
1. Pflug (West Germany)	1:31·4
2. Keulen-Deelstra (Holland)	1:31·6
3. Henning (USA)	1:31·6

1500 m

1. Holum (USA)	2:20·8
2. Baas-Kaiser (Holland)	2:21·0
3. Keulen-Deelstra (Holland)	2:22·0

3000 m

1. Baas-Kaiser (Holland)	4:52·1
2. Holum (USA)	4:58·6
3. Keulen-Deelstra (Holland)	4:59·9

Karl Schranz, the Austrian skier whose disqualification from the Sapporo Games for professionalism aroused a storm of controversy

FIGURE SKATING

Men	Points
1. Nepela (Czechoslovakia)	2739·1
2. Chetveroukhin (USSR)	2672·4
3. Pera (France)	2653·1

Women

1. Shuba (Austria)	2751·5
2. Magnussen (Canada)	2673·2
3. Lynn (USA)	2663·1

Pairs

1. Rodnina/Ulanov (USSR)	420·4
2. Smirnova/Souraikin (USSR)	419·4
3. Gross/Kagelmann (East Germany)	411·8

ICE HOCKEY

1. USSR
2. USA
3. Czechoslovakia

TOBOGGANING

Single-seater (men)	Minutes
1. Scheidel (East Germany)	3:27·58
2. Ehrig (East Germany)	3:28·39
3. Fiedler (East Germany)	3:28·73

Two-seater (men)

1. Italy (Hildgartner/Plaikner)	1:28·35
2. East Germany (Hornlein/Bredow)	1:28·35
3. East Germany (Bonsack/Fiedler)	1:29·16

Single-seater (women)

1. Muller (East Germany)	2:59·18
2. Ruhrold (East Germany)	2:59·49
3. Schumann (East Germany)	2:59·54

BOBSLED

Two-man

1. West Germany (Zimmerer/Utzschneider)	4:57·07
2. West Germany (Floth/Bader)	4:58·84
3. Switzerland (Wicki/Hubacher)	4:59·33

Four-man

1. Switzerland I	4:43·07
2. Italy I	4:43·83
3. West Germany I	4:43·92

A view of the impressive Olympic stadium during the opening ceremony at Munich

OLYMPIC GAMES IN MUNICH

ATHLETICS (MEN)

100 m	Seconds
1. Borzov (USSR)	10·14
2. Taylor (USA)	10·24
3. Miller (Jamaica)	10·33

200 m	
1. Borzov (USSR)	20·00
2. Black (USA)	20·19
3. Mennea (Italy)	20·30

400 m	
1. Matthews (USA)	44·66
2. Collett (USA)	44·80
3. Sang (Kenya)	44·92

800 m	Minutes
1. Wottle (USA)	1:45·9
2. Arzhanov (USSR)	1:45·9
3. Boit (Kenya)	1:46·0

1500 m	
1. Vasala (Finland)	3:36·3

Valeriy Borzov of the Soviet Union winning the gold medal for the 100 metres, the first Russian to win a gold in this event

2. Keino (Kenya)	3:36·8
3. Dixon (New Zealand)	3:37·5

5000 m

1. Viren (Finland)	13:26·4
2. Gammoudi (Tunisia)	13:27·4
3. Stewart (Great Britain)	13:27·6

10,000 m

1. Viren (Finland)	27:38·4
2. Puttemans (Belgium)	27:39·6
3. Yifter (Ethiopia)	27:41·0

Marathon	Hours
1. Shorter (USA)	2:12:19·8
2. Lismont (Belgium)	2:14:31·8
3. Wolde (Ethiopia)	2:15:08·4

110 m Hurdles	Seconds
1. Milburn (USA)	13·24
2. Drut (France)	13·34
3. Hill (USA)	13·48

400 m Hurdles

1. Akii-Bua (Uganda)	47·82
2. Mann (USA)	48·51
3. Hemery (Great Britain)	48·52

3000 m Steeplechase	Minutes
1. Keino (Kenya)	8:23·6
2. Jipcho (Kenya)	8:24·6
3. Kantanen (Finland)	8:24·8

4 × 100 (400) m Relay	Seconds
1. USA	38·19
2. USSR	38·50
3. West Germany	38·79

4 × 400 (1600) m Relay	Minutes
1. Kenya	2:59·8
2. Great Britain	3:00·5
3. France	3:00·7

20 km Walk	Hours
1. Frenkel (East Germany)	1:26:42·6
2. Golubnicki (USSR)	1:26:55·2
3. Reimann (East Germany)	1:27:16·6

50 km Walk

1. Kannenberg (West Germany)	3:56:11·6
2. Soldatenko (USSR)	3:58:24·0
3. Young (USA)	4:00:46·0

High Jump	Metres	
1. Tarmak (USSR)	2·23	(7′ 4″)
2. Junge (East Germany)	2·21	(7′ 3″)
3. Stones (USA)	2·21	(7′ 3″)

Long Jump

1. Williams (USA)	8·24	(27′ 0″)
2. Baumgartner (West Germany)	8·18	(26′ 10″)
3. Robinson (USA)	8·03	(26′ 4″)

Pole Vault

1. Nordwig (East Germany)	5·50	(18′ 0″)
2. Seagren (USA)	5·40	(17′ 9″)
3. Johnson (USA)	5·35	(17′ 7″)

Triple Jump

1. Saneyev (USSR)	17·35	(56′ 11″)
2. Drehmel (East Germany)	17·31	(56′ 9″)
3. Prudencio (Brazil)	17·05	(55′ 11″)

Shot Putt

1. Komar (Poland)	21·18	(69′ 6″)

2. Woods (USA)	21·17	(69′ 6″)
3. Briesenick (East Germany)	21·14	(69′ 4″)

Javelin

1. Wolfermann (West Germany)	90·48	(296′ 10″)
2. Lusis (USSR)	90·46	(296′ 9″)
3. Schmidt (USA)	84·42	(277′ 0″)

Discus

1. Danek (Czechoslovakia)	64·40	(211′ 3″)
2. Silvester (USA)	63·50	(208′ 4″)
3. Bruch (Sweden)	63·40	(208′ 0″)

Hammer

1. Bondarchuk (USSR)	75·50	(247′ 8″)
2. Sachse (East Germany)	74·96	(245′ 11″)
3. Khmelevski (USSR)	74·04	(242′ 11″)

Decathlon	Points
1. Avilov (USSR)	8454
2. Litvinenko (USSR)	8035
3. Katus (Poland)	7984

ATHLETICS (WOMEN)

100 m	Seconds
1. Stecher (East Germany)	11·07
2. Boyle (Australia)	11·23
3. Chivas (Cuba)	11·24

200 m	
1. Stecher (East Germany)	22·40
2. Boyle (Australia)	22·45
3. Szewinska (Poland)	22·74

400 m	
1. Zehrt (East Germany)	51·08
2. Wilden (West Germany)	51·21
3. Hammond (USA)	51·64

800 m	Minutes
1. Falck (West Germany)	1:58·6
2. Sabaite (USSR)	1:58·7
3. Hoffmeister (East Germany)	1:59·2

1500 m	
1. Bragina (USSR)	4:01·4
2. Hoffmeister (East Germany)	4:02·8
3. Cacchi (Italy)	4:02·9

100 m Hurdles	Seconds
1. Ehrhardt (East Germany)	12·59
2. Bufanu (Rumania)	12·84
3. Balzer (East Germany)	12·90

4 × 100 (400) m Relay	
1. West Germany	42·81
2. East Germany	42·95
3. Cuba	43·36

4 × 400 (1600) m Relay	Minutes
1. East Germany	3:23·0
2. USA	3:25·2
3. West Germany	3:26·5

High Jump	Metres	
1. Meyfarth (West Germany)	1·92	(6′ 4″)
2. Blagoeva (Bulgaria)	1·88	(6′ 2″)
3. Gusenbauer (Austria)	1·88	(6′ 2″)

Long Jump		
1. Rosendahl (West Germany)	6·78	(22′ 3″)
2. Yorgova (Bulgaria)	6·77	(22′ 3″)
3. Suranova (Czechoslovakia)	6·67	(21′ 11″)

America's Dave Wottle, his cap pulled tightly on to his head, appeared from nowhere to win the gold medal in the 800 metres from Russia's Evgeni Arzhanov and Kenya's Mike Boit. Wottle's was the first American gold medal in the 1972 Summer Games

Lasse Viren of Finland breasting the tape to win the 5000 metres from Mohamed Gammoudi of Tunisia and Ian Stewart of Britain. Viren, a policeman by profession, also won the 10,000 metres

Shot Putt

1. Chizhova (USSR)	21·03 (69′ 0″)
2. Gummel (East Germany)	20·22 (66′ 4″)
3. Christova (Bulgaria)	19·35 (63′ 6″)

Discus

1. Melnik (USSR)	66·62 (218′ 7″)
2. Menis (Rumania)	65·06 (213′ 5″)
3. Stoeva (Bulgaria)	64·34 (211′ 1″)

Javelin

1. Fuchs (East Germany)	63·88 (209′ 7″)
2. Todten (East Germany)	62·54 (205′ 2″)
3. Schmidt (USA)	59·94 (196′ 8″)

Pentathlon	Points
1. Peters (Great Britain)	4801
2. Rosendahl (West Germany)	4791
3. Pollak (East Germany)	4768

SWIMMING (MEN)

100 m Freestyle	Seconds
1. Spitz (USA)	51·22
2. Heidenreich (USA)	51·65
3. Bure (USSR)	51·77

200 m Freestyle	Minutes
1. Spitz (USA)	1:52·78
2. Genter (USA)	1:53·73
3. Lampe (West Germany)	1:53·99

400 m Freestyle

1. Demont (USA)*	4:00·26
2. Cooper (Australia)	4:00·27
3. Genter (USA)	4:01·94

1500 m Freestyle

1. Burton (USA)	15:52·58
2. Windeatt (Australia)	15:58·48
3. Northway (USA)	16:09·25

100 m Backstroke	Seconds
1. Matthes (East Germany)	56·58
2. Stamm (USA)	57·70
3. Murphy (USA)	58·35

200 m Backstroke	Minutes
1. Matthes (East Germany)	2:02·82
2. Stamm (USA)	2:04·09
3. Ivey (USA)	2:04·33

100 m Breaststroke

1. Taguchi (Japan)	1:04·94
2. Bruce (USA)	1:05·43
3. Hencken (USA)	1:05·61

200 m Breaststroke

1. Hencken (USA)	2:21·55
2. Wilkie (Great Britain)	2:23·67
3. Taguchi (Japan)	2:23·88

100 m Butterfly	Seconds
1. Spitz (USA)	54·27
2. Robertson (Canada)	55·56
3. Heidenreich (USA)	55·74

200 m Butterfly	Minutes
1. Spitz (USA)	2:00·70
2. Hall (USA)	2:02·86
3. Backhaus (USA)	2:03·23

200 m Individual Medley

1. Larsson (Sweden)	2:07·17
2. McKee (USA)	2:08·37
3. Furniss (USA)	2:08·45

Britain's Mary Peters putting the shot—one of the five events in the women's Pentathlon which she won, setting a world and Olympic record

400 m Individual Medley

1. Larsson (Sweden)	4:31·98
2. McKee (USA)	4:31·98
3. Hargitay (Hungary)	4:32·70

4 × 100 (400) m Freestyle Relay

1. USA	3:26·42
2. USSR	3:29·72
3. East Germany	3:32·42

4 × 200 (800) m Freestyle Relay

1. USA	7:35·78
2. West Germany	7:41·69
3. USSR	7:45·76

4 × 100 (400) m Medley Relay

1. USA	3:48·16
2. East Germany	3:52·12
3. Canada	3:52·26

Springboard Diving	Points
1. Vasin (USSR)	594·09
2. Cagnotto (Italy)	591·63
3. Lincoln (USA)	577·29

Platform Diving

1. Dibiasi (Italy)	504·12
2. Rydze (USA)	480·75
3. Cagnotto (Italy)	475·83

SWIMMING (WOMEN)

100 m Freestyle	Seconds
1. Neilson (USA)	58·59
2. Babashoff (USA)	59·02
3 Gould (Australia)	59·06

200 m Freestyle	Minutes
1. Gould (Australia)	2:03·56
2. Babashoff (USA)	2:04·33
3. Rothhammer (USA)	2:04·92

400 m Freestyle

1. Gould (Australia)	4:19·04
2. Calligaris (Italy)	4:22·44
3. Wegner (East Germany)	4:23·11

800 m Freestyle

1. Rothhammer (USA)	8:53·68
2. Gould (Australia)	8:56·39
3. Calligaris (Italy)	8:57·46

100 m Backstroke

1. Belote (USA)	1:05·78
2. Gyarmati (Hungary)	1:06·26
3. Atwood (USA)	1:06·34

200 m Backstroke

1. Belote (USA)	2:19·19
2. Atwood (USA)	2:20·38
3. Gurr (Canada)	2:23·22

100 m Butterfly

1. Aoki (Japan)	1:03·34
2. Beier (East Germany)	1:03·61
3. Gyarmati (Hungary)	1:03·73

200 m Butterfly

1. Moe (USA)	2:15·57
2. Colella (USA)	2:16·34
3. Daniel (USA)	2:16·74

100 m Breaststroke

1. Carr (USA)	1:13·58
2. Stepanova (USSR)	1:14·99
3. Whitfield (Australia)	1:15·73

200 m Breaststroke

1. Whitfield (Australia)	2:41·71
2. Schoenfield (USA)	2:42·05
3. Stepanova (USSR)	2:42·36

200 m Individual Medley

1. Gould (Australia)	2:23·07
2. Ender (East Germany)	2:23·59
3. Vidali (USA)	2:24·06

400 m Individual Medley

1. Neall (Australia)	5:02·97
2. Cliff (Canada)	5:03·57
3. Calligaris (Italy)	5:03·99

4 × 100 (400) m Freestyle Relay

1. USA	3:55·19
2. East Germany	3:55·55
3. West Germany	3:57·93

Mark Spitz of the United States—the wonder boy of the 1972 Olympics. Altogether he won seven gold medals for swimming—four individually, three in relay events—an Olympic record itself

Mid-action shot of Knape of Sweden in the women's platform diving event. She took the gold medal from the defending champion Milena Duchkova of Czechoslovakia

4 × 100 (400) m Medley Relay

1. USA	4:20·75
2. East Germany	4:24·91
3. West Germany	4:26·46

Springboard Diving	Points
1. King (USA)	450·03
2. Knape (Sweden)	434·19
3. Janicke (East Germany)	430·92

Platform Diving

1. Knape (Sweden)	390·00
2. Duchkova (Czechoslovakia)	370·92
3. Janicke (East Germany)	360·54

ROWING

Single Sculls	Minutes
1. Malishev (USSR)	7:10·12
2. Demiddi (Argentina)	7:11·53
3. Güldenpfennig (East Germany)	7:14·45

Double Sculls

1. USSR	7:01·77
2. Norway	7:02·58
3. East Germany	7:05·55

Coxswainless Pairs

1. East Germany	6:53·16
2. Switzerland	6:57·06
3. Holland	6:58·70

Coxed Pairs

1. East Germany	7:17·25
2. Czechoslovakia	7:19·57
3. Rumania	7:21·36

Coxswainless Fours

1. East Germany	6:24·27
2. New Zealand	6:25·64
3. West Germany	6:28·41

Coxed Fours

1. West Germany	6:31·85
2. East Germany	6:33·30
3. Czechoslovakia	6:35·64

Eights

1. New Zealand	6:08·94
2. USA	6:11·61
3. East Germany	6:11·67

YACHTING

Finn Class

1. Maury (France)
2. Hatzipavlis (Greece)
3. Potapov (USSR)

Flying Dutchman

1. Great Britain (Pattisson/Davies)
2. France (Pajot/Pajot)
3. West Germany (Libor/Naumann)

Star Class

1. Australia (Forbes/Anderson)
2. Sweden (Petterson/Westerdahl)
3. West Germany (Kuhweide/Meyer)

Dragon Class

1. Australia (Cuneo/Anderson/Shaw)
2. East Germany (Borowski/Weichert/Thun)
3. USA (Cohan/Horter/Marshall)

Tempest Class

1. USSR (Mankin/Dyrdyra)
2. Great Britain (Warren/Hunt)
3. USA (Foster/Dean)

Soling Class

1. USA (Melges/Bentsen/Allen)
2. Sweden (Wennerström/Knape/Krook)
3. Canada (Miller/Ekels/Cote)

The sailing events took place at Kiel on the Baltic Sea. Here, the Swedish Soling, S100, is in the lead before K93 of Great Britain. The Swedish team took the silver medal to the United States's gold

CANOEING (MEN)

Kayak Singles	Minutes
1. Shaparenko (USSR)	3:48·06
2. Peterson (Sweden)	3:48·35
3. Czapo (Hungary)	3:49·38

Kayak Pairs

1. USSR	3:31·23
2. Hungary	3:32·00
3. Poland	3:33·83

Kayak Fours

1. USSR	3:14·02
2. Rumania	3:15·07
3. Norway	3:15·27

Kayak Singles Slalom

1. Horn (East Germany)
2. Sattler (Austria)
3. Gimpel (East Germany)

Canadian Singles

1. Patzaichin (Rumania)	4:08·94
2. Wichmann (Hungary)	4:12·42
3. Lewe (West Germany)	4:13·63

Canadian Pairs

1. USSR	3:52·60
2. Rumania	3:52·63
3. Bulgaria	3:58·10

Canadian Singles Slalom

1. Eiben (East Germany)
2. Kauder (West Germany)
3. McEwan (USA)

Canadian Pairs Slalom

1. East Germany
2. West Germany
3. France

CANOEING (WOMEN)

Kayak Singles

1. Ryabchinskaya (USSR)	2:03·17
2. Jaapies (Holland)	2:04·03
3. Pfeffer (Hungary)	2:05·50

Kayak Pairs

1. USSR	1:53·50
2. East Germany	1:54·30
3. Rumania	1:55·01

Kayak Singles Slalom

1. Bahmann (East Germany)

2. Grothaus (West Germany)
3. Wunderlich (West Germany)

Swiss canoeist, Peter Daeni, negotiates a turn in the specially built kayak slalom course near Munich

BOXING

Light flyweight

1. Gedo (Hungary)
2. Kim (North Korea)
3. Evans (Great Britain)—Rodriguez (Spain)

Flyweight

1. Kostadinov (Bulgaria)
2. Rwabwogo (Uganda)
3. Blazynski (Poland)—Rodriguez (Cuba)

Bantamweight

1. Martinez (Cuba)
2. Zamora (Mexico)
3. Carreras (USA)—Turpin (Great Britain)

Featherweight

1. Kousnetsov (USSR)
2. Waruinge (Kenya)
3. Rojas (Colombia)—Botos (Hungary)

Lightweight

1. Szczepanski (Poland)
2. Orban (Hungary)
3. Perez (Colombia)—Mbugua (Kenya)

Light welterweight

1. Seales (USA)
2. Anghelov (Bulgaria)
3. Daborg (Nigeria)—Vujin (Yugoslavia)

Welterweight

1. Correa (Cuba)
2. Kajdi (Hungary)
3. Valdez (USA)—Murunga (Kenya)

Light middleweight

1. Kottysch (West Germany)
2. Rudkowski (Poland)
3. Minter (Great Britain)—Tiepold (East Germany)

Middleweight

1. Lemechev (USSR)

2. Virtanen (Finland)
3. Amartey (Ghana)—Johnson (USA)

Light heavyweight

1. Parlov (Yugoslavia)
2. Carrillo (Cuba)
3. Ikhouria (Nigeria)—Gortat (Poland)

Heavyweight

1. Stevenson (Cuba)
2. Alexe (Rumania)
3. Hussing (West Germany)—Thomson (Sweden)

CYCLING

1000 metres time trial	Minutes
1. Fredborg (Denmark)	1:06·44
2. Clark (Australia)	1:06·87
3. Schütze (East Germany)	1:07·02

1000 metres sprint

1. Morelon (France)
2. Nicholson (Australia)
3. Phakadze (USSR)

2000 metres tandem

1. USSR (Semenez/Zelovalnikov)
2. East Germany (Geschke/Otto)
3. Poland (Bek/Kocot)

4000 metres team pursuit

1. West Germany	4:22·14
2. East Germany	4:25·25
3. Great Britain	4:25·78

4000 metres individual pursuit

1. Knudsen (Norway)	4:45·74
2. Kurmann (Switzerland)	4:51·96
3. Lutz (West Germany)	4:50·80

100 km road team time trial

1. USSR	2:11:17·8
2. Poland	2:11:47·5
3. Holland	2:12:27·1

Individual road race

1. Kuiper (Holland)	4:14:37·0
2. Sefton (Australia)	4:15:04·0
3. Huelamo (Spain)	4:15:04·0

WRESTLING—GRECO-ROMAN

Paperweight

1. Berceanu (Rumania)
2. Aliabadi (Iran)
3. Anghelov (Bulgaria)

Flyweight

1. Kirov (Bulgaria)
2. Hirayama (Japan)
3. Bognanni (Italy)

Bantamweight

1. Kazakov (USSR)
2. Veil (West Germany)
3. Bjoerlin (Finland)

Featherweight

1. Markov (Bulgaria)
2. Wehling (East Germany)
3. Lipien (Poland)

Lightweight

1. Khisamutdinov (USSR)
2. Apostolov (Bulgaria)
3. Ranzi (Italy)

Welterweight

1. Macha (Czechoslovakia)

The presence of armed guards in the Olympic Village stressed the ugly political atmosphere which overshadowed the Munich games

2. Galaktopoulos (Greece)
3. Karlsson (Sweden)

Middleweight

1. Hegedus (Hungary)
2. Nazarenko (USSR)
3. Nenadic (Yugoslavia)

Light heavyweight

1. Rezantsev (USSR)
2. Corak (Yugoslavia)
3. Kwiecinski (Poland)

Heavyweight

1. Martinescu (Rumania)
2. Jakovenko (USSR)
3. Kiss (Hungary)

Extra heavyweight

1. Roshin (USSR)
2. Tomov (Bulgaria)
3. Dolipschi (Rumania)

WRESTLING—FREESTYLE

Paperweight

1. Dmitriev (USSR)
2. Nikolov (Bulgaria)
3. Javadpour (Iran)

Flyweight

1. Kato (Japan)
2. Alakhverdiev (USSR)
3. Kim Gwong (North Korea)

Bantamweight

1. Yanagida (Japan)
2. Sanders (USA)
3. Klinga (Hungary)

Featherweight

1. Abdulbekov (USSR)
2. Akdag (Turkey)
3. Krastev (Bulgaria)

Lightweight

1. Gable (USA)
2. Wada (Japan)
3. Ashuraliev (USSR)

Welterweight

1. Wells (USA)
2. Karlsson (Sweden)
3. Seger (West Germany)

Middleweight

1. Tediashvili (USSR)
2. J. Peterson (USA)
3. Jorga (Rumania)

Light heavyweight

1. B. Peterson (USA)
2. Strakhov (USSR)
3. Bajko (Hungary)

Heavyweight

1. Yarygin (USSR)
2. Baianmunkh (Mongolia)
3. Csatari (Hungary)

Extra heavyweight

1. Medved (USSR)
2. Douraliev (Bulgaria)
3. Taylor (USA)

JUDO

Lightweight

1. Kawaguchi (Japan)
2. Buidaa (Mongolia)*
3. Kim (North Korea)—Mounier (France)

Welterweight

1. Nomura (Japan)
2. Zajkowski (Poland)
3. Hötger (East Germany)—Novikov (USSR)

Middleweight

1. Sekine (Japan)
2. Oh (South Korea)
3. Jacks (Great Britain)—Coche (France)

Light heavyweight

1. Chochoshvili (USSR)
2. Starbrook (Great Britain)
3. Ishii (Brazil)—Barth (West Germany)

Heavyweight

1. Ruska (Holland)
2. Glahn (West Germany)
3. Onashvili (USSR)—Nishimura (Japan)

Open Class

1. Ruska (Holland)
2. Kusnetzov (USSR)
3. Brondani (France)—Parisi (Great Britain)

GYMNASTICS (MEN)

Combined exercises—team	Points
1. Japan	571·25
2. USSR	564·05
3. East Germany	559·70

Combined exercises—individual	
1. Kato (Japan)	114·650
2. Kenmotsu (Japan)	114·575
3. Nakayama (Japan)	114·325

Horizontal bar	
1. Tsukahara (Japan)	19·725
2. Kato (Japan)	19·525
3. Kasamatsu (Japan)	19·450

Parallel bars	
1. Kato (Japan)	19·475
2. Kasamatsu (Japan)	19·375
3. Kenmotsu (Japan)	19·250

Rings	
1. Nakayama (Japan)	19·350
2. Voronin (USSR)	19·275
3. Tsukahara (Japan)	19·225

Floor exercises	
1. Andrianov (USSR)	19·175
2. Nakayama (Japan)	19·125
3. Kasamatsu (Japan)	19·025

Pommelled horse	
1. Klimenko (USSR)	19·125
2. Kato (Japan)	19·000
3. Kenmotsu (Japan)	18·950

Long horse vault	
1. Köste (East Germany)	18·850
2. Klimenko (USSR)	18·825
3. Andrianov (USSR)	18·800

GYMNASTICS (WOMEN)

Combined exercises—team	
1. USSR	380·50
2. East Germany	376·55
3. Hungary	368·25

Combined exercises—individual	
1. Tourischeva (USSR)	77·025

For the first time, archery was an Olympic event in 1972. The winner of the first gold medal was John Williams of the United States

2. Janz (East Germany)	76·875
3. Lazakovitsch (USSR)	76·850

Asymmetrical bars

1. Janz (East Germany)	19·675
2. Korbut (USSR)	19·450
3. Zuchold (East Germany)	19·450

Beam

1. Korbut (USSR)	19·400
2. Lazakovitsch (USSR)	19·375
3. Janz (East Germany)	18·975

Horse vault

1. Janz (East Germany)	19·525
2. Zuchold (East Germany)	19·275
3. Tourischeva (USSR)	19·250

Floor exercises

1. Korbut (USSR)	19·575
2. Tourischeva (USSR)	19·550
3. Lazakovitsch (USSR)	19·450

WEIGHTLIFTING

Flyweight	Kgs	(lbs)
1. Smalcerz (Poland)	337·5	(744)
2. Szuecs (Hungary)	330·0	(727½)
3. Holczreiter (Hungary)	327·5	(722)

Bantamweight

1. Foeldi (Hungary)	377·5	(832¼)
2. Nassiri (Iran)	370·0	(815¾)
3. Chetin (USSR)	367·5	(810¼)

Featherweight

1. Nourikian (Bulgaria)	402·5	(887¼)
2. Shanidze (USSR)	400·0	(881¾)
3. Benedek (Hungary)	390·0	(859¾)

Lightweight

1. Kirzhinov (USSR)	460·0	(1014¼)
2. Koutchev (Bulgaria)	450·0	(992)
3. Kaczmarek (Poland)	437·5	(964½)

Middleweight

1. Bikov (Bulgaria)	485·0	(1069¼)
2. Trabulsi (Lebanon)	472·5	(1041¾)
3. Silvino (Italy)	470·0	(1036¼)

Light heavyweight

1. Jenssen (Norway)	507·5	(1118¾)
2. Ozimek (Poland)	497·5	(1096¾)
3. Horvath (Hungary)	495·0	(1091¼)

Middle heavyweight

1. Nikolov (Bulgaria)	525·0	(1157½)
2. Chopov (Bulgaria)	517·5	(1140¾)
3. Bettembourg (Sweden)	512·5	(1129¾)

Heavyweight

1. Talts (USSR)	580·0	(1278¾)
2. Kraitchev (Bulgaria)	562·5	(1240)
3. Grützner (East Germany)	555·0	(1223½)

Extra heavyweight

1. Alexeiev (USSR)	640·0	(1411)
2. Mang (West Germany)	610·0	(1344¾)
3. Bonk (East Germany)	572·5	(1262¼)

SHOOTING

Free rifle (three positions)	Points
1. Wigger (USA)	1155
2. Melnik (USSR)	1155
3. Pap (Hungary)	1149

Small-bore rifle (three positions)

1. Writer (USA)	1166
2. Bassham (USA)	1157
3. Lippoldt (East Germany)	1153

Small-bore rifle (prone)

1. Jun Li (North Korea)	599
2. Auer (USA)	598
3. Rotaru (Rumania)	598

Free pistol

1. Skanaker (Sweden)	567
2. Iuga (Rumania)	562
3. Dollinger (Austria)	560

Rapid-fire pistol

1. Zapedzki (Poland)	595
2. Faita (Czechoslovakia)	594
3. Torshin (USSR)	593

Clay pigeon (Trap)

1. Scalzone (Italy)	199
2. Carrega (France)	198
3. Basagni (Italy)	195

Skeet

1. Wirnhier (West Germany)	195
2. Petrov (USSR)	195
3. Buchheim (East Germany)	195

Moving target

1. Zhelezniak (USSR)	569
2. Bellingrodt (Colombia)	565
3. Kynoch (Great Britain)	562

ARCHERY

Women

1. Wilber (USA)	2424

2. Szydlowska (Poland)	2407
3. Gapchenko (USSR)	2403

Men

1. Williams (USA)	2528
2. Jarvil (Sweden)	2481
3. Laasonen (Finland)	2467

FENCING

Team foil (women)

1. USSR
2. Hungary
3. Rumania

Individual foil (women)

1. Ragno-Lonzi (Italy)
2. Bobis (Hungary)
3. Gorokhova (USSR)

Team foil (men)

1. Poland
2. USSR
3. France

Individual foil (men)

1. Woyda (Poland)
2. Kamuti (Hungary)
3. Noel (France)

Team épée

1. Hungary
2. Switzerland
3. USSR

Individual épée

1. Fenyvesi (Hungary)
2. La Degaillerie (France)
3. Kulcsar (Hungary)

Team sabre

1. Italy
2. USSR
3. Hungary

Individual sabre

1. Sidiak (USSR)
2. Maroth (Hungary)
3. Nazlymov (USSR)

MODERN PENTATHLON

Individual

1. Balczo (Hungary)	5412
2. Onischenko (USSR)	5335
3. Lednev (USSR)	5328

Team

1. USSR	15·968
2. Hungary	15·348
3. Finland	14·812

RIDING

Three-day event (individual)

1. Meade (Great Britain)	57·73
2. Argenton (Italy)	43·33
3. Jonsson (Sweden)	39·67

Three-day event (team)

1. Great Britain	95·53
2. USA	110·81
3. West Germany	118·00

Dressage—individual

1. Linsenhoff (West Germany)	1229·00
2. Petushkova (USSR)	1185·00
3. Neckermann (West Germany)	1177·00

Dressage—team

1. USSR	5095·0
2. West Germany	5083·0
3. Sweden	4849·0

Grand Prix jumping—individual

1. Mancinelli (Italy)
2. Moore (Great Britain)
3. Shapiro (USA)

Grand Prix jumping—team

1. West Germany
2. USA
3. Italy

TEAM SPORTS

Water polo

1. USSR
2. Hungary
3. USA

Hockey

1. West Germany
2. Pakistan
3. India

Britain's Mary Gordon Watson, one of the team which won the three-day equestrian event

The retiring President of the International Olympic Committee, Avery Brundage, leads the applause at a press conference for his successor, Lord Killanin

Volleyball (women)

1. USSR
2. Japan
3. North Korea

Volleyball (men)

1. Japan
2. East Germany
3. USSR

Basketball

1. USSR
2. USA
3. Cuba

Football

1. Poland
2. Hungary
3. East Germany—USSR

Handball

1. Yugoslavia
2. Czechoslovakia
3. Rumania

* *Positive results on dope testing—medal forfeited.*

As the Olympic flame flares and dies on the last day of the Munich Games, the thanks of millions are expressed to Avery Brundage on the giant electronic scoreboard

OLYMPIC CHAMPIONS SINCE 1896

CELEBRATIONS OF THE MODERN OLYMPIC GAMES

I.	Athens	1896	VIII.	Paris	1924	XV.	Helsinki	1952
II.	Paris	1900	IX.	Amsterdam	1928	XVI.	Melbourne	1956
III.	St Louis	1904	X.	Los Angeles	1932	XVII.	Rome	1960
IV.	London	1908	XI.	Berlin	1936	XVIII.	Tokyo	1964
V.	Stockholm	1912	XII.	Tokyo/Helsinki*	1940	XIX.	Mexico City	1968
VI.	Berlin*	1916	XIII.	London*	1944			
VII.	Antwerp	1920	XIV.	London	1948			

*cancelled due to World War

ATHLETICS (MEN)

100 m

1896	Burke (USA)	12·0
1900	Jarvis (USA)	11·0
1904	Hahn (USA)	11·0
1908	Walker (S. Africa)	10·8
1912	Craig (USA)	10·8
1920	Paddock (USA)	10·8
1924	Abrahams (Great Britain)	10·6
1928	Williams (Canada)	10·8
1932	Tolan (USA)	10·3
1936	Owens (USA)	10·3
1948	Dillard (USA)	10·3
1952	Remigino (USA)	10·4
1956	Morrow (USA)	10·5
1960	Hary (West Germany)	10·2
1964	Hayes (USA)	10·0
1968	Hines (USA)	9·9

200 m

1896	Event not held	
1900	Tewksbury (USA)	22·2
1904	Hahn (USA)	21·6
1908	Kerr (Canada)	22·6
1912	Craig (USA)	21·7
1920	Woodring (USA)	22·0
1924	Scholz (USA)	21·6
1928	Williams (Canada)	21·8
1932	Tolan (USA)	21·2
1936	Owens (USA)	20·7
1948	Patton (USA)	21·1
1952	Stanfield (USA)	20·7
1956	Morrow (USA)	20·6
1960	Berruti (Italy)	20·5
1964	Carr (USA)	20·3
1968	Smith (USA)	19·8

400 m

1896	Burke (USA)	54·2
1900	Long (USA)	49·4
1904	Hillman (USA)	49·2
1908	Halswelle (Great Britain)	50·0
1912	Reidpath (USA)	48·2
1920	Rudd (S. Africa)	49·6
1924	Liddell (Great Britain)	47·6
1928	Barbuti (USA)	47·8
1932	Carr (USA)	46·2
1936	Williams (USA)	46·5
1948	Wint (Jamaica)	46·2
1952	Rhoden (Jamaica)	45·9
1956	Jenkins (USA)	46·7
1960	Davis (USA)	44·9
1964	Larrabee (USA)	45·1
1968	Evans (USA)	43·8

800 m

1896	Flack (Australia)	2:11·0
1900	Tysoe (Great Britain)	2:01·2
1904	Lightbody (USA)	1:56·0
1908	Sheppard (USA)	1:52·8
1912	Meredith (USA)	1:51·9
1920	Hill (Great Britain)	1:53·4
1924	Lowe (Great Britain)	1:52·4
1928	Lowe (Great Britain)	1:51·8
1932	Hampson (Great Britain)	1:49·8
1936	Woodruff (USA)	1:52·9
1948	Whitfield (USA)	1:49·2
1952	Whitfield (USA)	1:49·2
1956	Courtney (USA)	1:47·7
1960	Snell (New Zealand)	1:46·3
1964	Snell (New Zealand)	1:45·1
1968	Doubell (Australia)	1:44·3

1500 m

1896	Flack (Australia)	4:33·2
1900	Bennett (Great Britain)	4:06·0
1904	Lightbody (USA)	4:05·4
1908	Sheppard (USA)	4:03·4
1912	Jackson (Great Britain)	3:56·8
1920	Hill (Great Britain)	4:01·8
1924	Nurmi (Finland)	3:53·6
1928	Larva (Finland)	3:53·2
1932	Beccali (Italy)	3:51·2
1936	Lovelock (New Zealand)	3:47·8
1948	Eriksson (Sweden)	3:49·8
1952	Barthel (Luxemburg)	3:45·2
1956	Delany (Ireland)	3:41·2
1960	Elliott (Australia)	3:35·6
1964	Snell (New Zealand)	3:38·1
1968	Keino (Kenya)	3:34·9

5000 m

1896–1908	Event not held	
1912	Kolehmainen (Finland)	14:36·6
1920	Guillemot (France)	14:55·6
1924	Nurmi (Finland)	14:31·2
1928	Ritola (Finland)	14:38·0
1932	Lehtinen (Finland)	14:30·0
1936	Höckert (Finland)	14:22·2
1948	Reiff (Belgium)	14:17·6
1952	Zatopek (Czechoslovakia)	14:06·6
1956	Kuts (USSR)	13:39·6
1960	Halberg (New Zealand)	13:43·4
1964	Schul (USA)	13:48·8
1968	Gammoudi (Tunisia)	14:05·0

10,000 m

1896–1908	Event not held	
1912	Kolehmainen (Finland)	31:20·8
1920	Nurmi (Finland)	31:45·8
1924	Ritola (Finland)	30:23·2
1928	Nurmi (Finland)	30:18·8
1932	Kusocinski (Poland)	30:11·4
1936	Salminen (Finland)	30:15·4
1948	Zatopek (Czechoslovakia)	29:59·6
1952	Zatopek (Czechoslovakia)	29:17·0
1956	Kuts (USSR)	28:45·6
1960	Bolotnikov (USSR)	28:32·2
1964	Mills (USA)	28:24·4
1968	Temu (Kenya)	29:27·4

Marathon

1896	Louis (Greece)	2:58:50·0
1900	Théato (France)	2:59:45·0
1904	Hicks (USA)	3:28:53·0
1908	Hayes (USA)	2:55:18·4
1912	McArthur (S. Africa)	2:36:54·8
1920	Kolehmainen (Finland)	2:32:35·8
1924	Stenroos (Finland)	2:41:22·6
1928	El Ouafi (France)	2:32:57·0
1932	Zabala (Argentina)	2:31:36·0
1936	Son (Japan)	2:29:19·2
1948	Cabrera (Argentina)	2:34:51·6
1952	Zatopek (Czechoslovakia)	2:23:03·2
1956	Mimoun (France)	2:25:00·0
1960	Bikila (Ethiopia)	2:15:16·2
1964	Bikila (Ethiopia)	2:12:11·2
1968	Wolde (Ethiopia)	2:20:26·4

110 m Hurdles

1896	Curtis (USA) (only 100 m)	17·6
1900	Kraenzlein (USA)	15·4
1904	Schule (USA)	16·0
1908	Smithson (USA)	15·0
1912	Kelly (USA)	15·1
1920	Thomson (Canada)	14·8

1924	Kinsey (USA)	15·0
1928	Atkinson (S. Africa)	14·8
1932	Saling (USA)	14·6
1936	Towns (USA)	14·2
1948	Porter (USA)	13·9
1952	Dillard (USA)	13·7
1956	Calhoun (USA)	13·5
1960	Calhoun (USA)	13·8
1964	Jones (USA)	13·6
1968	Davenport (USA)	13·3

400 m Hurdles

1896	Event not held	
1900	Tewksbury (USA)	57·6
1904	Hillman (USA)	*53·0
1908	Bacon (USA)	55·0
1912	Event not held	
1920	Loomis (USA)	54·0
1924	Taylor (USA)	52·6
1928	Burghley (Great Britain)	53·4
1932	Tisdall (Ireland)	51·8
1936	Hardin (USA)	52·4
1948	Cochran (USA)	51·1
1952	Moore (USA)	50·8
1956	Davis (USA)	50·1
1960	Davis (USA)	49·3
1964	Cawley (USA)	49·6
1968	Hemery (Great Britain)	48·1
	* Hurdles only 2′ 6″ high	

3000 m Steeplechase

1896	Event not held	
1900–1908	Held over different distances	
1912	Event not held	
1920	Hodge (Great Britain)	10:00·4
1924	Ritola (Finland)	9:33·6
1928	Loukola (Finland)	9:21·8
1932	Iso-Hollo (Finland)	*10:33·4
1936	Iso-Hollo (Finland)	9:03·8
1948	Sjöstrand (Sweden)	9:04·6
1952	Ashenfelter (USA)	8:45·4
1956	Brasher (Great Britain)	8:41·2
1960	Krzyszkowiak (Poland)	8:34·2
1964	Roelants (Belgium)	8:30·8
1968	Biwott (Kenya)	8:51·0
	* extra leg run in error	

4 × 100 (400) m Relay

1896–1908	Event not held	
1912	Great Britain	42·4
1920	USA	42·2
1924	USA	41·0
1928	USA	41·0
1932	USA	40·0
1936	USA	39·8
1948	USA	40·6
1952	USA	40·1
1956	USA	39·5
1960	Germany	39·5
1964	USA	39·0
1968	USA	38·2

4 × 400 (1600) m Relay

1896–1908	Event not held	
1912	USA	3:16·6
1920	Great Britain	3:22·2
1924	USA	3:16·0
1928	USA	3:14·2
1932	USA	3:08·2
1936	Great Britain	3:09·0
1948	USA	3:10·4
1952	Jamaica	3:03·9
1956	USA	3:04·8
1960	USA	3:02·2
1964	USA	3:00·7
1968	USA	2:56·1

20 km Walk

1896–1952	Event not held	
1956	Spirin (USSR)	1:31:27·4
1960	Golubnichiy (USSR)	1:34:07·2
1964	Matthews (Great Britain)	1:29:34·0
1968	Golubnichiy (USSR)	1:33:58·4

50 km Walk

1896–1928	Event not held	
1932	Green (Great Britain)	4:50:10·0
1936	Whitlock (Great Britain)	4:30:41·4
1948	Ljunggren (Sweden)	4:41:52·0
1952	Dordoni (Italy)	4:28:07·8
1956	Read (New Zealand)	4:30:42·8
1960	Thompson (Great Britain)	4:25:30·0
1964	Pamich (Italy)	4:11:12·4
1968	Höhne (East Germany)	4:20:13·6

High Jump

1896	Clark (USA)	5′ 11¼″
1900	Baxter (USA)	6′ 2¾″
1904	Jones (USA)	5′ 11″
1908	Porter (USA)	6′ 3″
1912	Richards (USA)	6′ 4″
1920	Landon (USA)	6′ 4⅜″
1924	Osborn (USA)	6′ 6″
1928	King (USA)	6′ 4⅜″
1932	McNaughton (Canada)	6′ 5½″
1936	Johnson (USA)	6′ 7⅞″
1948	Winter (Australia)	6′ 6″
1952	Davis (USA)	6′ 8⅜″
1956	Dumas (USA)	6′ 11½″
1960	Schavlakadze (USSR)	7′ 1⅛″
1964	Brumel (USSR)	7′ 1¾″
1968	Fosbury (USA)	7′ 4¼″

Long Jump

1896	Clark (USA)	20′ 10″
1900	Kraenzlein (USA)	23′ 6⅞″
1904	Prinstein (USA)	24′ 1″
1908	Irons (USA)	24′ 6½″
1912	Gutterson (USA)	24′ 11¼″
1920	Pettersson (Sweden)	23′ 5½″
1924	Hubbard (USA)	24′ 5″
1928	Hamm (USA)	25′ 4¼″
1932	Gordon (USA)	25′ 0¾″
1936	Owens (USA)	26′ 5¼″
1948	Steele (USA)	25′ 8″
1952	Biffle (USA)	24′ 10″
1956	Bell (USA)	25′ 8¼″
1960	Boston (USA)	26′ 7½″
1964	Davies (Great Britain)	26′ 5¾″
1968	Beamon (USA)	29′ 2½″

Pole Vault

1896	Hoyt (USA)	10′ 10″
1900	Baxter (USA)	10′ 10″
1904	Dvorak (USA)	11′ 6″
1908	Cooke and Gilbert (USA) – tie	12′ 2″
1912	Babcock (USA)	12′ 11½″
1920	Foss (USA)	13′ 5″
1924	Barnes (USA)	12′ 11½″
1928	Carr (USA)	13′ 9¼″
1932	Miller (USA)	14′ 1⅞″
1936	Meadows (USA)	14′ 3¼″
1948	Smith (USA)	14′ 1¼″
1952	Richards (USA)	14′ 11¼″
1956	Richards (USA)	14′ 11½″
1960	Bragg (USA)	15′ 5″
1964	Hansen (USA)	16′ 8¾″
1968	Seagren (USA)	17′ 8½″

Triple Jump

1896	Connolly (USA)	44′ 11¾″
1900	Prinstein (USA)	47′ 5¾″
1904	Prinstein (USA)	47′ 1″
1908	Ahearne (Great Britain)	48′ 11¼″
1912	Lindblom (Sweden)	48′ 5″
1920	Tuulos (Finland)	47′ 7″
1924	Winter (Australia)	50′ 11¼″
1928	Oda (Japan)	49′ 10¾″
1932	Nambu (Japan)	51′ 7″
1936	Tajima (Japan)	52′ 6″
1948	Ahman (Sweden)	50′ 6¼″
1952	da Silva (Brazil)	53′ 2½″
1956	da Silva (Brazil)	53′ 7¾″
1960	Schmidt (Poland)	55′ 1¾″
1964	Schmidt (Poland)	55′ 3½″
1968	Sanejev (USSR)	57′ 0¾″

Shot Putt

1896	Garrett (USA)	36′ 9¾″
1900	Sheldon (USA)	46′ 3″
1904	Rose (USA)	48′ 7″
1908	Rose (USA)	46′ 7½″
1912	McDonald (USA)	50′ 4″
1920	Pörhölä (Finland)	48′ 7″
1924	Houser (USA)	49′ 2¼″
1928	Kuck (USA)	52′ 0¾″

1932	Sexton (USA)	52′ 6⅛″
1936	Woellke (Germany)	53′ 1¾″
1948	Thompson (USA)	56′ 2″
1952	O'Brien (USA)	57′ 1½″
1956	O'Brien (USA)	60′ 11¼″
1960	Nieder (USA)	65′ 6¾″
1964	Long (USA)	66′ 8½″
1968	Matson (USA)	67′ 4¾″

Javelin

1896–1904	Event not held	
1908	Lemming (Sweden)	179′ 10½″
1912	Lemming (Sweden)	198′ 11¼″
1920	Myyrä (Finland)	215′ 9½″
1924	Myyrä (Finland)	206′ 6½″
1928	Lundquist (Sweden)	218′ 6″
1932	Järvinen (Finland)	238′ 6½″
1936	Stöck (Germany)	235′ 8½″
1948	Rautavaara (Finland)	228′ 11″
1952	Young (USA)	242′ 0½″
1956	Danielsen (Norway)	281′ 2¼″
1960	Zybulenko (USSR)	277′ 8¼″
1964	Nevala (Finland)	271′ 2″
1968	Lusis (USSR)	295′ 7″

Discus

1896	Garrett (USA)	95′ 7¾″
1900	Bauer (Hungary)	118′ 3″
1904	Sheridan (USA)	128′ 10½″
1908	Sheridan (USA)	134′ 2″
1912	Taipale (Finland)	148′ 4″
1920	Niklander (Finland)	146′ 7¼″
1924	Houser (USA)	151′ 5″
1928	Houser (USA)	155′ 3″
1932	Anderson (USA)	162′ 4½″
1936	Carpenter (USA)	165′ 7½″
1948	Consolini (Italy)	172′ 2″
1952	Iness (USA)	180′ 6½″
1956	Oerter (USA)	184′ 11″
1960	Oerter (USA)	194′ 1¾″
1964	Oerter (USA)	200′ 1½″
1968	Oerter (USA)	212′ 6½″

Hammer

1896	Event not held	
1900	Flanagan (USA)	163′ 2″
1904	Flanagan (USA)	168′ 1″
1908	Flanagan (USA)	170′ 4¼″
1912	McGrath (USA)	179′ 7″
1920	Ryan (USA)	173′ 5½″
1924	Tootell (USA)	174′ 10″
1928	O'Callaghan (Ireland)	168′ 7″
1932	O'Callaghan (Ireland)	176′ 11″
1936	Hein (Germany)	185′ 4″
1948	Nemeth (Hungary)	183′ 11½″
1952	Csermak (Hungary)	197′ 11½″
1956	Connolly (USA)	207′ 3½″
1960	Rudenkov (USSR)	220′ 1¾″
1964	Klim (USSR)	228′ 10½″
1968	Zsivotzky (Hungary)	240′ 8″

Decathlon

		Points*
1896–1900	Event not held	
1904	Kiely (Great Britain)	6036
1908	Event not held	
1912	Wieslander (Sweden)	7724·49
1920	Lövland (Norway)	6804·35
1924	Osborn (USA)	7710·77
1928	Yrjölä (Finland)	8053·29
1932	Bausch (USA)	8462·23
1936	Morris (USA)	7900
1948	Mathias (USA)	7139
1952	Mathias (USA)	7887
1956	Campbell (USA)	7937
1960	Johnson (USA)	8392
1964	Holdorf (West Germany)	7887
1968	Toomey (USA)	8193

* old scoring system up to 1960

ATHLETICS (WOMEN)

100 m

1928	Robinson (USA)	12·2
1932	Walasiewicz (Poland)	11·9
1936	Stephens (USA)	11·5
1948	Blankers-Koen (Netherlands)	11·9
1952	Jackson (Australia)	11·5
1956	Cuthbert (Australia)	11·5
1960	Rudolph (USA)	11·0
1964	Tyus (USA)	11·4
1968	Tyus (USA)	11·0

200 m

1928–1936	Event not held	
1948	Blankers-Koen (Netherlands)	24·4
1952	Jackson (Australia)	23·7
1956	Cuthbert (Australia)	23·4
1960	Rudolph (USA)	24·0
1964	McGuire (USA)	23·0
1968	Szewinska (Poland)	22·5

400 m

1928–1960	Event not held	
1964	Cuthbert (Australia)	52·0
1968	Besson (France)	52·0

800 m

1928	Radke-Batschauer (Germany)	2:16·8
1932–1956	Event not held	
1960	Schevzova (USSR)	2:04·3
1964	Packer (Great Britain)	2:01·1
1968	Manning (USA)	2:00·9

80 m Hurdles

1928	Event not held	
1932	Didrikson (USA)	11·7
1936	Valla (Italy)	11·7
1948	Blankers-Koen (Netherlands)	11·2
1952	Strickland (Australia)	10·9
1956	Strickland (Australia)	10·7
1960	I. Press (USSR)	10·8
1964	Balzer (East Germany)	10·5
1968	Caird (Australia)	10·3

4 × 100 (400) m Relay

1928	Canada	48·4
1932	USA	47·0
1936	USA	46·9
1948	Netherlands	47·5
1952	USA	45·9
1956	Australia	44·5
1960	USA	44·5
1964	Poland	43·6
1968	USA	42·8

High jump

1928	Catherwood (Canada)	5′ 2⅝″
1932	Shiley (USA)	5′ 5″
1936	Csak (Hungary)	5′ 3″
1948	Coachman (USA)	5′ 6⅛″
1952	Brand (S. Africa)	5′ 5¾″
1956	McDaniel (USA)	5′ 9¼″
1960	Balas (Rumania)	6′ 0⅞″
1964	Balas (Rumania)	6′ 2¾″
1968	Rezkova (Czechoslovakia)	5′ 11⅝″

Long jump

1928–1936	Event not held	
1948	Gyarmati (Hungary)	18′ 8¼″
1952	Williams (New Zealand)	20′ 5⅝″
1956	Krzesinska (Poland)	20′ 10″
1960	Krepkina (USSR)	20′ 10¾″
1964	Rand (Great Britain)	22′ 2¼″
1968	Viscopoleanu (Rumania)	22′ 4½″

Shot putt

1928–1936	Event not held	
1948	Ostermeyer (France)	45′ 1½″
1952	Zybina (USSR)	50′ 1½″
1956	Tyschkevitsch (USSR)	54′ 5″
1960	T. Press (USSR)	56′ 10″
1964	T. Press (USSR)	59′ 6″
1968	Gummel (East Germany)	64′ 4″

Discus

1928	Konopacka (Poland)	129′ 11¾″
1932	Copeland (USA)	133′ 1¾″
1936	Mauermayer (Germany)	156′ 3¼″
1948	Ostermeyer (France)	137′ 6⅛″
1952	Romaschkova (USSR)	168′ 8½″
1956	Fikotova (Czechoslovakia)	176′ 1½″
1960	Ponomaryeva (USSR)	180′ 9¼″
1964	T. Press (USSR)	187′ 10½″
1968	Manoliu (Rumania)	191′ 2½″

Javelin

1928	Event not held	
1932	Didrikson (USA)	143′ 4″
1936	Fleischer (Germany)	148′ 2¾″
1948	Bauma (Austria)	149′ 6″
1952	Zatopekova (Czechoslovakia)	165′ 7″
1956	Jaunseme (USSR)	176′ 8½″
1960	Ozolina (USSR)	183′ 8″
1964	Penes (Rumania)	198′ 7½″
1968	Nemeth (Hungary)	198′ 0½″

Pentathlon (with 80 m Hurdles)

		Points
1928–1960	Event not held	
1964	I. Press (USSR)	5246
1968	Becker (West Germany)	5098

SWIMMING (MEN)

100 m Freestyle

1896	Hajos (Hungary)	1:22·2
1900	Event not held	
1904	Halmay (Hungary) (100 Yards)	1:02·8
1908	Daniels (USA)	1:05·6
1912	Kahanamoku (USA)	1:03·4
1920	Kahanamoku (USA)	1:00·4
1924	Weissmuller (USA)	59·0
1928	Weissmuller (USA)	58·6
1932	Miyazaki (Japan)	58·2
1936	Csik (Hungary)	57·6
1948	Ris (USA)	57·3
1952	Scholes (USA)	57·4
1956	Henricks (Australia)	55·4
1960	Devitt (Australia)	55·2
1964	Schollander (USA)	53·4
1968	Wenden (Australia)	52·2

200 m Freestyle

1896	Event not held	
1900	Lane (Australia)	2:25·2
1904	Daniels (USA) 220 Yards	2:44·2
1908–1964	Event not held	
1968	Wenden (Australia)	1:55·2

400 m Freestyle

1896	Neumann (Austria) 500 m	8:12·6
1900	Event not held	
1904	Daniels (USA) 440 Yards	6:16·2
1908	Taylor (Great Britain)	5:36·8
1912	Hodgson (Canada)	5:24·4
1920	Ross (USA)	5:26·8
1924	Weissmuller (USA)	5:04·2
1928	Zorilla (Argentina)	5:01·6
1932	Crabbe (USA)	4:48·4
1936	Medica (USA)	4:44·5
1948	Smith (USA)	4:41·0
1952	Boiteux (France)	4:30·7
1956	Rose (Australia)	4:27·3
1960	Rose (Australia)	4:18·3
1964	Schollander (USA)	4:12·2
1968	Burton (USA)	4:09·0

1500 m Freestyle

1896–1904	Event not held	
1908	Taylor (Great Britain)	22:48·4
1912	Hodgson (Canada)	22:00·0
1920	Ross (USA)	22:23·2
1924	Charlton (Australia)	20:06·6
1928	Borg (Sweden)	19:51·8
1932	Kitamura (Japan)	19:12·4
1936	Terada (Japan)	19:13·7
1948	McLane (USA)	19:18·5
1952	Konno (USA)	18:30·3
1956	Rose (Australia)	17:58·9
1960	Konrads (Australia)	17:19·6
1964	Windle (Australia)	17:01·7
1968	Burton (USA)	16:39·9

100 m Backstroke

1904	Brack (Germany) (100 Yards)	1:16·8
1908	Bieberstein (Germany)	1:24·6
1912	Hebner (USA)	1:21·2
1920	Kealoha (USA)	1:15·2
1924	Kealoha (USA)	1:13·2
1928	Kojac (USA)	1:08·2
1932	Kiyokawa (Japan)	1:08·6
1936	Kiefer (USA)	1:05·9
1948	Stack (USA)	1:06·4
1952	Oyakawa (Japan)	1:05·4
1956	Theile (Australia)	1:02·2
1960	Theile (Australia)	1:01·9
1964	Event not held	
1968	Matthes (East Germany)	58·7

200 m Backstroke

1900	Hoppenberg (Germany)	2:47·0
1904–1960	Event not held	
1964	Graef (USA)	2:10·3
1968	Matthes (East Germany)	2:09·6

100 m Breaststroke

1968	McKenzie (USA)	1:07·7

200 m Breaststroke

1908	Holman (Great Britain)	3:09·2
1912	Bathe (Germany)	3:01·8
1920	Malmroth (Sweden)	3:04·4
1924	Skelton (USA)	2:56·6
1928	Tsuruta (Japan)	2:48·8
1932	Tsuruta (Japan)	2:45·4
1936	Hamuro (Japan)	2:41·5
1948	Verdeur (USA)	2:39·3
1952	Davies (Australia)	2:34·4
1956	Furukawa (Japan)	2:34·7
1960	Mulliken (USA)	2:37·4
1964	O'Brien (Australia)	2:27·8
1968	Munoz (Mexico)	2:28·7

100 m Butterfly

1968	Russel (USA)	55·9

200 m Butterfly

1956	Yorzyk (USA)	2:19·3
1960	Troy (USA)	2:12.8
1964	Berry (Australia)	2:06·6
1968	Robie (USA)	2:08·7

200 m Individual Medley

1968	Hickcox (USA)	2:12·0

400 m Individual Medley

1964	Roth (USA)	4:45·4
1968	Hickcox (USA)	4:48·4

Springboard Diving

		Points
1908	Zürner (Germany)	85·50
1912	Günther (Germany)	79·23
1920	Kuehn (USA)	675·00
1924	White (USA)	696·40
1928	Desjardins (USA)	185·04
1932	Galitzen (USA)	161·38
1936	Degener (USA)	163·57
1948	Harlan (USA)	163·64
1952	Browning (USA)	205·29
1956	Clotworthy (USA)	159·56
1960	Tobian (USA)	170·00
1964	Sitzberger (USA)	159·90
1968	Wrightson (USA)	170·14

Platform Diving

1904	Sheldon (USA) (combined event)	12·75
1908	Johansson (Sweden)	83·75
1912	Adlerz (Sweden)	73·94
1920	Pinkston (USA)	100·67
1924	White (USA)	97·46
1928	Desjardins (USA)	98·74
1932	Smith (USA)	124·80
1936	Wayne (USA)	113·58
1948	Lee (USA)	130·05
1952	Lee (USA)	156·28
1956	Capilla (Mexico)	152·44
1960	Webster (USA)	165·56
1964	Webster (USA)	148·58
1968	Dibiasi (Italy)	164·18

4 × 100 (400) m Freestyle Relay

1964	USA	3:33·2
1968	USA	3:31·7

4 × 200 (800) m Freestyle Relay

1908	Great Britain	10:55·6
1912	Australia	10:11·2
1920	USA	10:04·4
1924	USA	9:53·4
1928	USA	9:36·2
1932	Japan	8:58·4

1936	Japan	8:51·5
1948	USA	8:46·0
1952	USA	8:31·1
1956	Australia	8:23·6
1960	USA	8:10·2
1964	USA	7:52·1
1968	USA	7:52·3

4 × 100 (400) m Medley Relay

1960	USA	4:05·4
1964	USA	3:58·5
1968	USA	3:54·9

SWIMMING (WOMEN)

100 m Freestyle

1912	Durack (Australia)	1:22·2
1920	Bleibtrey (USA)	1:13·6
1924	Lackie (USA)	1:12·4
1928	Osipowich (USA)	1:11·0
1932	Madison (USA)	1:06·8
1936	Mastenbroek (Netherlands)	1:05·9
1948	Andersen (Denmark)	1:06·3
1952	Szoke (Hungary)	1:06·8
1956	Fraser (Australia)	1:02·0
1960	Fraser (Australia)	1:01·2
1964	Fraser (Australia)	59·5
1968	Henne (USA)	1:00·0

200 m Freestyle

1968	Meyer (USA)	2:10·5

400 m Freestyle

1920	Bleibtrey (USA) (300 m)	4:34·0
1924	Norelius (USA)	6:02·2
1928	Norelius (USA)	5:42·8
1932	Madison (USA)	5:28·5
1936	Mastenbroek (Netherlands)	5:26·4
1948	Curtis (USA)	5:17·8
1952	Gyenge (Hungary)	5:12·1
1956	Crapp (Australia)	4:54·6
1960	von Saltza (USA)	4:50·5
1964	Duenkel (USA)	4:43·3
1968	Meyer (USA)	4:31.8

800 m Freestyle

1968	Meyer (USA)	9:24·0

100 m Backstroke

1924	Bauer (USA)	1:23·2
1928	Braun (Netherlands)	1:22·0
1932	Holm (USA)	1:19·4
1936	Senff (Netherlands)	1:18·9
1948	Harup (Denmark)	1:14·4
1952	Harrison (S. Africa)	1:14·3
1956	Grinham (Great Britain)	1:12·9
1960	Burke (USA)	1:09·3
1964	Ferguson (USA)	1:07·7
1968	Hall (USA)	1:06·2

200 m Backstroke

1968	Watson (USA)	2:24·8

100 m Butterfly

1956	Mann (USA)	1:11·0
1960	Schuler (USA)	1:09·5
1964	Stouder (USA)	1:04·7
1968	McClements (Australia)	1:05·5

200 m Butterfly

1968	Kok (Netherlands)	2:24·7

100 m Breaststroke

1968	Bjedov (Yugoslavia)	1:15·8

200 m Breaststroke

1924	Morton (Great Britain)	3:33·2
1928	Schrader (Germany)	3:12·6
1932	Dennis (Australia)	3:06·3
1936	Maehata (Japan)	3:03·6
1948	van Vliet (Netherlands)	2:57·2
1952	Szekely (Hungary)	2:51·7
1956	Happe (West Germany)	2:53·1
1960	Lonsbrough (Great Britain)	2:49·5
1964	Prosumenschikova (USSR)	2:46·4
1968	Wichman (USA)	2:44·4

200 m Individual Medley

1968	Kolb (USA)	2:24·7

400 m Individual Medley

1964	de Varona (USA)	5:18·7
1968	Kolb (USA)	5:08·5

4 × 100 (400) m Freestyle Relay

1912	Great Britain	5:52·8
1920	USA	5:11·6
1924	USA	4:58·8
1928	USA	4:47·6
1932	USA	4:38·0
1936	Netherlands	4:36·0
1948	USA	4:29·2
1952	Hungary	4:24·4
1956	Australia	4:17·1
1960	USA	4:08·9
1964	USA	4:03·8
1968	USA	4:02·5

4 × 100 (400) m Medley Relay

1960	USA	4:41·1
1964	USA	4:33·9
1968	USA	4:28·3

Springboard Diving		Points
1920	Riggin (USA)	539·90
1924	Becker (USA)	474·50
1928	Meany (USA)	78·62
1932	Coleman (USA)	87·52
1936	Gestring (USA)	89·27
1948	Draves (USA)	108·74
1952	McCormick (USA)	147·30
1956	McCormick (USA)	142·36
1960	Krämer (West Germany)	155·81
1964	Engel-Krämer (West Germany)	145·00
1968	Gossick (USA)	150·67

Platform Diving

1912	Johansson (Sweden)	39·90
1920	Fryland-Clausen (Denmark)	34·60
1924	Smith (USA)	33·20
1928	Pinkston (USA)	31·60
1932	Poynton (USA)	40·26
1936	Hill-Poynton (USA)	33·93
1948	Draves (USA)	68·87
1952	McCormick (USA)	79·37
1956	McCormick (USA)	84·85
1960	Krämer (West Germany)	155·81
1964	Bush (USA)	99·80
1968	Duchkova (Czechoslovakia)	109·59

ROWING

Single Sculls

1900	Barrelet (France)	7:35·6
1904	Greer (USA)	10:08·5
1908	Blackstaffe (Great Britain)	9:26·0
1912	Kinnear (Great Britain)	7:47·6
1920	Kelly (USA)	7:35·0
1924	Beresford (Great Britain)	7:49·2
1928	Pearce (Australia)	7:11·0
1932	Pearce (Australia)	7:44·4
1936	Schäfer (Germany)	8:21·5
1948	Wood (Australia)	7:24·4
1952	Tschukalov (USSR)	8:12·8
1956	Ivanov (USSR)	8:02·5
1960	Ivanov (USSR)	7:13·96
1964	Ivanov (USSR)	8:22·51
1968	Wienese (Netherlands)	7:47·80

Double Sculls

1904	USA	10:03·25
1908–1912	Event not held	
1920	USA	7:09·0
1924	USA	7:45·0
1928	USA	6:41·4
1932	USA	7:17·4
1936	Great Britain	7:20·8
1948	Great Britain	6:51·3
1952	Argentina	7:32·2
1956	USSR	7:24·0
1960	Czechoslovakia	6:47·50
1964	USSR	7:10·66
1968	USSR	6:51·82

Coxswainless Pairs

1900	Belgium	
1904	USA	10:57·0
1908	Great Britain	9:41·0

1912	Event not held	
1920	Italy	7:56·0
1924	Netherlands	8:19·4
1928	Germany	7:06·4
1932	Great Britain	8:00·0
1936	Germany	8:16·1
1948	Great Britain	7:21·1
1952	USA	8:20·7
1956	USA	7:55·4
1960	USSR	7:02·01
1964	Canada	7:32·94
1968	East Germany	7:26·56

Coxed Pairs

1900	Netherlands	7:34·2
1904–1920	Event not held	
1924	Switzerland	8:39·0
1928	Switzerland	7:42·6
1932	USA	8:25·8
1936	Germany	8:36·9
1948	Denmark	8:00·5
1952	France	8:28·6
1956	USA	8:26·1
1960	Germany	7:29·14
1964	USA	8:21·33
1968	Italy	8:04·81

Coxswainless Fours

1900	France	7:11·0
1904	USA	9:53·8
1908	Great Britain	8:34·0
1912–1920	Event not held	
1924	Great Britain	7:08·6
1928	Great Britain	6:36·0
1932	Great Britain	6:58·2
1936	Germany	7:01·8
1948	Italy	6:39·0
1952	Yugoslavia	7:16·0
1956	Canada	7:08·8
1960	USA	6:26·26
1964	Denmark	6:59·30
1968	East Germany	6:39·18

Coxed Fours

1900	Germany	5:59·0
1904	USA	
1908	Event not held	
1912	Germany	6:59·4
1920	Switzerland	6:54·0
1924	Switzerland	7:18·4
1928	Italy	6:47·8
1932	Germany	7:19·0
1936	Germany	7:16·2
1948	USA	6:50·3
1952	Czechoslovakia	7:33·4
1956	Italy	7:19·4
1960	West Germany	6:39·12
1964	West Germany	7:00·44
1968	New Zealand	6:45·42

Eights

1900	USA	6:09·8
1904	USA	7:50·0
1908	Great Britain	7:52·0
1912	Great Britain	6:15·0
1920	USA	6:02·6
1924	USA	6:33·4
1928	USA	6:03·2
1932	USA	6:37·6
1936	USA	6:25·4
1948	USA	5:56·7
1952	USA	6:25·9
1956	USA	6:35·2
1960	West Germany	5:57·18
1964	USA	6:18·23
1968	West Germany	6:07·00

YACHTING

5·5 m Class

1952	USA	5751
1956	Sweden	5527
1960	USA	6055
1964	Australia	5981
1968	Sweden	8·0

Dragon Class

1948	Norway	4746
1952	Norway	6130
1956	Sweden	5723
1960	Greece	6715
1964	Denmark	5854
1968	USA	6·0

Star Class

1932	USA	46
1936	Germany	80
1948	USA	5828
1952	Italy	7635
1956	USA	5876
1960	USSR	7619
1964	Bahamas	5664
1968	USA	14·4

Flying Dutchman

1960	Norway	6774
1964	New Zealand	6255
1968	Great Britain	3·0

Finn Class

1956	Elvström (Denmark)	7509
1960	Elvström (Denmark)	8171
1964	Kuhweide (West Germany)	7638
1968	Mankin (USSR)	11·7

CANOEING (MEN)

Kayak Singles

1936	Hradetzky (Austria)	4:22·9
1948	Fredriksson (Sweden)	4:33·2
1952	Fredriksson (Sweden)	4:07·9
1956	Fredriksson (Sweden)	4:12·8
1960	Hansen (Denmark)	3:53·00
1964	Pettersson (Sweden)	3:37·13
1968	Hesz (Hungary)	4:02·36

Kayak Pairs

1936	Austria	4:03·8
1948	Sweden	4:07·3
1952	Finland	3:51·1
1956	West Germany	3:49·6
1960	Sweden	3:34·73
1964	Sweden	3:38·54
1968	USSR	3:37·54

Kayak Fours

1964	USSR	3:14·67
1968	Norway	3:14·38

Canadian Singles

1936	Amyot (Canada)	5:32·1
1948	Holecek (Czechoslovakia)	5:42·0
1952	Holecek (Czechoslovakia)	4:56·3
1956	Rottman (Rumania)	5:05·3
1960	Parti (Hungary)	4:33·93
1964	Eschert (West Germany)	4:35·14
1968	Tatai (Hungary)	4:36·14

Canadian Pairs

1936	Czechoslovakia	4:50·1
1948	Czechoslovakia	5:07·1
1952	Denmark	4:38·3
1956	Rumania	4:47·4
1960	USSR	4:17·93
1964	USSR	4:04·65
1968	Rumania	4:07·18

CANOEING (WOMEN)

Kayak Singles

1948	Hoff (Denmark)	2:31·9
1952	Saimo (Finland)	2:18·4
1956	Dementjeva (USSR)	2:18·9
1960	Seredina (USSR)	2:08·08
1964	Khvedosiuk (USSR)	2:12·87
1968	Pinajeva (USSR)	2:11·09

Kayak Pairs

1960	USSR	1:54·76
1964	West Germany	1:56·95
1968	West Germany	1:56·44

BOXING

Light flyweight

1968	Rodriguez (Venezuela)	

Flyweight
1904 Finnegan (USA)
1908–1912 Event not held
1920 de Genero (USA)
1924 La Barba (USA)
1928 Kocsis (Hungary)
1932 Enekes (Hungary)
1936 Kaiser (Germany)
1948 Perez (Argentina)
1952 Brooks (USA)
1956 Spinks (Great Britain)
1960 Török (Hungary)
1964 Atzori (Italy)
1968 Delgado (Mexico)

Bantamweight
1904 Kirk (USA)
1908 Thomas (Great Britain)
1912 Event not held
1920 Walker (S. Africa)
1924 Smith (S. Africa)
1928 Tamagnini (Italy)
1932 Gwynne (Canada)
1936 Sergo (Italy)
1948 Csik (Hungary)
1952 Hämäläinen (Finland)
1956 Behrendt (West Germany)
1960 Grigoryev (USSR)
1964 Sakurai (Japan)
1968 Sokolov (USSR)

Featherweight
1904 Kirk (USA)
1908 Gunn (Great Britain)
1912 Event not held
1920 Fritsch (France)
1924 Fields (USA)
1928 van Klaveren (Netherlands)
1932 Robledo (Argentina)
1936 Casanovas (Argentina)
1948 Formenti (Italy)
1952 Zachara (Czechoslovakia)
1956 Safronov (USSR)
1960 Musso (Italy)
1964 Stepaschkin (USSR)
1968 Roldan (Mexico)

Lightweight
1904 Spanger (USA)
1908 Grace (Great Britain)
1912 Event not held
1920 Mosberg (USA)
1924 Nielsen (Denmark)
1928 Orlandi (Italy)
1932 Stevens (S. Africa)
1936 Harangi (Hungary)
1948 Dreyer (S. Africa)
1952 Bolognesi (Italy)
1956 McTaggart (Great Britain)
1960 Pazdzior (Poland)
1964 Grudzien (Poland)
1968 Harris (USA)

Light welterweight
1952 Adkins (USA)
1956 Jengibarjan (USSR)
1960 Nemecek (Czechoslovakia)
1964 Kulej (Poland)
1968 Kulej (Poland)

Welterweight
1904 Young (USA)
1908—1912 Event not held
1920 Schneider (Canada)
1924 Delarge (Belgium)
1928 Morgan (New Zealand)
1932 Flynn (USA)
1936 Suvio (Finland)
1948 Torma (Czechoslovakia)
1952 Chychla (Poland)
1956 Linca (Rumania)
1960 Benvenuti (Italy)
1964 Kasprzyk (Poland)
1968 Wolke (East Germany)

Light middleweight
1952 Papp (Hungary)
1956 Papp (Hungary)
1960 McClure (USA)
1964 Lagutin (USSR)
1968 Lagutin (USSR)

Middleweight
1904 Mayer (USA)
1908 Douglas (Great Britain)
1912 Event not held
1920 Mallin (Great Britain)
1924 Mallin (Great Britain)
1928 Toscani (Italy)
1932 Barth (USA)
1936 Despeaux (France)
1948 Papp (Hungary)
1952 Patterson (USA)
1956 Schatkov (USSR)
1960 Crook (USA)
1964 Popenschenko (USSR)
1968 Finnegan (Great Britain)

Light heavyweight
1920 Eagan (USA)
1924 Mitchell (Great Britain)
1928 Avendano (Argentina)
1932 Carstens (S. Africa)
1936 Michelot (France)
1948 Hunter (S. Africa)
1952 Lee (USA)
1956 Boyd (USA)
1960 Clay (USA)
1964 Pinto (Italy)
1968 Posnjak (USSR)

Heavyweight
1904 Berger (USA)
1908 Oldman (Great Britain)
1912 Event not held
1920 Rawson (Great Britain)
1924 von Porath (Northway)
1928 Jurado (Argentina)
1932 Lovell (Argentina)
1936 Runge (Germany)
1948 Iglesias (Argentina)
1952 Sanders (USA)
1956 Rademacher (USA)
1960 de Piccoli (Italy)
1964 Frazier (USA)
1968 Forman (USA)

CYCLING

1,000 metres time trial

1928	Falck-Hansen (Denmark)	1:14·4
1932	Gray (Australia)	1:13·0
1936	van Vliet (Netherlands)	1:12·0
1948	Dupont (France)	1:13·5
1952	Mockridge (Australia)	1:11·1
1956	Faggin (Italy)	1:09·8
1960	Gaiardoni (Italy)	1:07·3
1964	Sercu (Belgium)	1:09·59
1968	Trentin (France)	1:03·91

1,000 metres sprint
1896 Masson (France)
1900 Taillandier (France)
1904 Event not held
1908 Race declared void
1912 Event not held
1920 Peeters (Netherlands)
1924 Michard (France)
1928 Beaufrand (France)
1932 van Egmond (Netherlands)
1936 Merkens (Germany)
1952 Sacchi (Italy)
1956 Rousseau (France)
1948 Ghella (Italy)
1960 Gaiardoni (Italy)
1964 Pettenella (Italy)
1968 Morelon (France)

2,000 metres tandem
1908 France (Schilles/Auffray)
1912 Event not held
1920 Great Britain (Ryan/Lance)
1924 France (Choury/Cugnot)
1928 Netherlands (Leene/van Dijk)
1932 France (Perrin/Chaillot)

1936	Germany (Ihbe/Lorenz)	
1948	Italy (Perona/Teruzzi)	
1952	Australia (Mockridge/Cox)	
1956	Australia (Browne/Marchant)	
1960	Italy (Beghetto/Bianchetto)	
1964	Italy (Bianchetto/Damiano)	
1968	France (Morelon/Tretin)	

4,000 metres team pursuit

1900	USA (1,500 m)	2:17·2
1908	Great Britain (1,810 m)	2:18·6
1912	Event not held	
1920	Italy	5:20·0
1924	Italy	5:15·0
1928	Italy	5:01·8
1932	Italy	4:53·0
1936	France	4:45·0
1948	France	4:57·8
1952	Italy	4:46·1
1956	Italy	4:47·4
1960	Italy	4:30·9
1964	West Germany	4:34·67
1968	Denmark	4:22·44

4,000 metres individual pursuit

1964	Daler (Czechoslovakia)	5:04·75
1968	Rebillard (France)	4:41·71

Road team time trial

1912 Sweden
1920 France
1924 France
1928 Denmark
1932 Italy
1936 France
1948 Belgium
1952 Belgium
1956 France
1960 Italy
1964 Netherlands
1968 Netherlands

Road race

1896 Konstantinides (Greece)
1900 Event not held
1904 Downing (USA)
1908 Bartlett (Great Britain)
1912 Lewis (S. Africa)
1920 Stenquist (Sweden)
1924 Blanchonnet (France)
1928 Hansen (Denmark)
1932 Pavesi (Italy)
1936 Charpentier (France)
1948 Beyaert (France)
1952 Noyelle (Belgium)
1956 Baldini (Italy)
1960 Kapitonov (USSR)
1964 Zanin (Italy)
1968 Vianelli (Italy)

WRESTLING – GRECO-ROMAN

Flyweight

1932 Brendel (Germany)
1936 Lörincz (Hungary)
1948 Lombardi (Italy)
1952 Gurevitsch (USSR)
1956 Solovyev (USSR)
1960 Pirvulescu (Rumania)
1964 Hanahara (Japan)
1968 Kiroff (Bulgaria)

Bantamweight

1924 Püttsepp (Estonia)
1928 Leucht (Germany)
1932 Gozzi (Italy)
1936 Erkan (Turkey)
1948 Petersson (Sweden)
1952 Hodos (Hungary)
1956 Vyrupayev (USSR)
1960 Karavayev (USSR)
1964 Ishigushi (Japan)
1968 Varga (Hungary)

Featherweight

1912 Koskelo (Finland)
1920 Friman (Finland)
1924 Anttila (Finland)
1928 Wäli (Estonia)
1932—1936 Event not held
1948 Oktav (Turkey)
1952 Punkin (USSR)
1956 Mäkinen (Finland)
1960 Sille (Turkey)
1964 Polyak (Hungary)
1968 Rurua (USSR)

Lightweight

1908 Porro (Italy)
1912 Väre (Finland)
1920 Väre (Finland)
1924 Friman (Finland)
1928 Keresztes (Hungary)
1932 Malmberg (Sweden)
1936 Koskela (Finland)
1948 Freij (Sweden)
1952 Safin (USSR)
1956 Lehtonen (Finland)
1960 Koridse (USSR)
1964 Ayvas (Turkey)
1968 Mumemura (Japan)

Welterweight

1928 Kokkinen (Finland)
1932 Johansson (Sweden)
1936 Svedberg (Sweden)
1948 Andersson (Sweden)
1952 Szilvasi (Hungary)
1956 Bayrak (Turkey)
1960 Bayrak (Turkey)
1964 Kolesov (USSR)
1968 Vesper (East Germany)

Middleweight

1908 Martensson (Sweden)
1912 Johansson (Sweden)
1920 Westergren (Sweden)
1924 Westerlund (Finland)
1928 Moustafa (Egypt)
1932 Kokkinen (Finland)
1936 Johansson (Sweden)
1948 Grönberg (Sweden)
1952 Grönberg (Sweden)
1956 Kartosija (USSR)
1960 Dobreff (Bulgaria)
1964 Simic (Yugoslavia)
1968 Metz (East Germany)

Light heavyweight

1908 Weckman (Finland)
1912 Ahlgren (Sweden), Bohling (Finland) – tie
1920 Johansson (Sweden)
1924 Westergren (Sweden)
1928 Event not held
1932 Svensson (Sweden)
1936 Cadier (Sweden)
1948 Nilsson (Sweden)
1952 Gröndahl (Finland)
1956 Nikolayev (USSR)
1960 Kis (Turkey)
1964 Alexandroff (Bulgaria)
1968 Radeff (Bulgaria)

Heavyweight

1896 Schumann (Germany)
1900—1904 Event not held
1908 Weisz (Hungary)
1912 Saarela (Finland)
1920 Lindfors (Finland)
1924 Deglane (France)
1928 Svensson (Sweden)
1932 Westergren (Sweden)
1936 Palusalu (Estonia)
1948 Kirecci (Turkey)
1952 Kotkas (USSR)
1956 Parfenov (USSR)
1960 Bogdan (USSR)
1964 Kozma (Hungary)
1968 Kozma (Hungary)

WRESTLING – FREESTYLE

Flyweight

1904 Curry (USA)
1908–1936 Event not held
1948 Vitala (Finland)

1952 Gemici (Turkey)
1956 Zalkalamanidse (USSR)
1960 Bilek (Turkey)
1964 Yoshida (Japan)
1968 Nakata (Japan)

Bantamweight
1904 Mehnert (USA)
1908 Mehnert (USA)
1912—1920 Event not held
1924 Pihlajamäki (Finland)
1928 Mäkinen (Finland)
1932 Pearce (USA)
1936 Zombori (Hungary)
1948 Akar (Turkey)
1952 Ishii (Japan)
1956 Dagistanli (Turkey)
1960 McCann (USA)
1964 Uetake (Japan)
1968 Uetake (Japan)

Featherweight
1904 Niflot (USA)
1908 Dole (USA)
1912 Event not held
1920 Ackerly (USA)
1924 Reed (USA)
1928 Morrison (USA)
1932 Pihlajamäki (Finland)
1936 Pihlajamäki (Finland)
1948 Bilge (Turkey)
1952 Sit (Turkey)
1956 Sasahara (Japan)
1960 Dagistanli (Turkey)
1964 Watanabe (Japan)
1968 Kaneko (Japan)

Lightweight
1904 Bradshaw (USA)
1908 de Relwyskow (Great Britain)
1912 Event not held
1920 Anttila (Finland)
1924 Vis (USA)
1928 Käpp (Estonia)
1932 Pacome (France)
1936 Karpati (Hungary)
1948 Atik (Turkey)
1952 Anderberg (Sweden)
1956 Habibi (Iran)
1960 Wilson (USA)
1964 Dimoff (Bulgaria)
1968 Mohaved (Iran)

Welterweight
1924 Gehri (Switzerland)
1928 Haavisto (Finland)
1932 van Bebber (USA)
1936 Lewis (USA)
1948 Dogu (Turkey)
1952 Smith (USA)
1956 Ikeda (Japan)
1960 Blubaugh (USA)
1964 Ogan (Turkey)
1968 Atalay (Turkey)

Middleweight
1904 Roem (USA)
1908 Bacon (Great Britain)
1912 Event not held
1920 Leino (Finland)
1924 Haggmann (Switzerland)
1928 Kyburz (Switzerland)
1932 Johansson (Sweden)
1936 Poilve (France)
1948 Brand (USA)
1952 Zimakuridse (USSR)
1956 Nikoloff (Bulgaria)
1960 Güngör (Turkey)
1964 Gardieff (Bulgaria)
1968 Gurevitsch (USSR)

Light heavyweight
1904 Erickson (USA)
1908—1912 Event not held
1920 Larsson (Sweden)
1924 Spellman (USA)
1928 Sjöstedt (Sweden)
1932 Mehringer (USA)
1936 Fridell (Sweden)
1948 Wittenberg (USA)
1952 Palm (Sweden)
1956 Takhti (Iran)
1960 Athli (Turkey)
1964 Medwed (USSR)
1968 Ayik (Turkey)

Heavyweight
1904 Hansen (USA)
1908 O'Kelly (Great Britain)
1912 Event not held
1920 Roth (Switzerland)
1924 Steele (USA)
1928 Richthoff (Sweden)
1932 Richthoff (Sweden)
1936 Palusalu (Estonia)
1948 Bobis (Hungary)
1952 Mekokischvili (USSR)
1956 Kaplan (Turkey)
1960 Dietrich (West Germany)
1964 Ivanitsky (USSR)
1968 Medwed (USSR)

GYMNASTICS (MEN)

Combined exercises – team		Points
1904	USA	374·43
1908	Sweden	438·00
1912	Italy	265·75
1920	Italy	359·85
1924	Italy	839·05
1928	Switzerland	1718·62
1932	Italy	541·85
1936	Germany	657·43
1948	Finland	1358·30
1952	USSR	574·40
1956	USSR	568·25
1960	Japan	575·20
1964	Japan	577·95
1968	Japan	575·90

Combined exercises – individual		
1900	Sandras (France)	320
1904	Heida (USA)	161
1908	Braglia (Italy)	317
1912	Braglia (Italy)	135
1920	Zampori (Italy)	88·35
1924	Stukelij (Yugoslavia)	110·34
1928	Miez (Switzerland)	247·62
1932	Neri (Italy)	140·62
1936	Schwarzmann (Germany)	113·10
1948	Huhtanen (Finland)	229·7
1952	Tschukarin (USSR)	115·70
1956	Tschukarin (USSR)	114·25
1960	Schaklin (USSR)	115·95
1964	Endo (Japan)	115·95
1968	Kato (Japan)	115·90

Horizontal bar		
1896	Weingärtner (Germany)	
1900	Event not held	
1904	Heida and Henning (of USA)—tie	40
1908–1920	Event not held	
1924	Stukelij (Yugoslavia)	19·37
1928	Miez (Switzerland)	19·17
1932	Bixler (USA)	18·33
1936	Saarvala (Finland)	19·36
1948	Stalder (Switzerland)	39·7
1952	Günthard (Switzerland)	19·55
1956	Ono (Japan)	19·60
1960	Ono (Japan)	19·60
1964	Schaklin (USSR)	19·625
1968	Nakayama (Japan)	19·550

Parallel bars		
1896	Flatow (Germany)	
1900	Event not held	
1904	Eyser (USA)	44
1908–1920	Event not held	
1924	Güttinger (Switzerland)	21·63
1928	Vacha (Czechoslovakia)	18·83
1932	Neri (Italy)	18·97
1936	Frey (Germany)	19·07
1948	Reusch (Switzerland)	39·5
1952	Eugster (Switzerland)	19·65
1956	Tschukarin (USSR)	19·20
1960	Schaklin (USSR)	19·40

1964	Endo (Japan)	19·675
1968	Nakayama (Japan)	19·550

Rings

1896	Mitropoulos (Greece)	
1900	Event not held	
1904	Glass (USA)	45
1908–1920	Event not held	
1924	Martino (Italy)	21·55
1928	Stukelij (Yugoslavia)	19·25
1932	Gulack (USA)	18·97
1936	Hudec (Czechoslovakia)	19·43
1948	Frei (Switzerland)	39·6
1952	Schaginjan (USSR)	19·75
1956	Asarjan (USSR)	19·35
1960	Asarjan (USSR)	19·725
1964	Hayata (Japan)	19·475
1968	Nakayama (Japan)	19·450

Floor exercises

1932	Pelle (Hungary)	28·8
1936	Miez (Switzerland)	18·66
1948	Pataki (Hungary)	38·7
1952	Thoresson (Sweden)	19·25
1956	Muratov (USSR)	19·20
1960	Aihara (Japan)	19·45
1964	Menichelli (Italy)	19·450
1968	Kato (Japan)	19·475

Pommelled horse

1896	Zutter (Switzerland)	
1900	Event not held	
1904	Heida (USA)	42
1908–1920	Event not held	
1924	Wilhelm (Switzerland)	21·23
1928	Hänggi (Switzerland)	19·75
1932	Pelle (Hungary)	19·07
1936	Frey (Germany)	19·33
1948	Aaltonen, Huhtanen, Savolainen (Finland)—tie	38·7
1952	Tschukarin (USSR)	19·50
1956	Schaklin (USSR)	19·25
1960	Schaklin (USSR)	19·375
1964	Cerar (Yugoslavia)	19·525
1968	Cerar (Yugoslavia)	19·325

Long horse vault

1896	Schumann (Germany)	
1900	Event not held	
1904	Heida and Eyser (of USA)—tie	36
1908–1920	Event not held	
1924	Kriz (USA)	9·98
1928	Mack (Switzerland)	9·58
1932	Guglielmetti (Italy)	18·03
1936	Schwarzmann (Germany)	19·20
1948	Aaltonen (Finland)	39·10
1952	Tschukarin (USSR)	19·20
1956	Bantz (West Germany) and Muratov (USSR)—tie	18·85
1960	Ono (Japan)	19·350
1964	Yamashita (Japan)	19·600
1968	Voronin (USSR)	19·000

GYMNASTICS (WOMEN)

Combined exercises – team

1928	Netherlands	316·75
1932	Event not held	
1936	Germany	506·50
1948	Czechoslovakia	445·45
1952	USSR	527·03
1956	USSR	444·80
1960	USSR	382·320
1964	USSR	380·890
1968	USSR	382·850

Combined exercises – individual

1952	Gorochovskaja (USSR)	76·78
1956	Latynina (USSR)	74·933
1960	Latynina (USSR)	77·031
1964	Caslavska (Czechoslovakia)	77·564
1968	Caslavska (Czechoslovakia)	78·250

Parallel bars

1952	Korondi (Hungary)	19·40
1956	Keleti (Hungary)	18·966
1960	Astachova (USSR)	19·616
1964	Astachova (USSR)	19·332
1968	Caslavska (Czechoslovakia)	19·650

Beam

1952	Botscharova (USSR)	19·22
1956	Keleti (Hungary)	18·799
1960	Bosakova (Czechoslovakia)	19·283
1964	Caslavska (Czechoslovakia)	19·449
1968	Kutschinskaja (USSR)	19·650

Horse vault

1952	Kalintschuk (USSR)	19·20
1956	Latynina (USSR)	18·833
1960	Nikolajeva (USSR)	19·316
1964	Caslavska (Czechoslovakia)	19·483
1968	Caslavska (Czechoslovakia)	19·775

Floor exercises

1952	Keleti (Hungary)	19·36
1956	Keleti (Hungary) and Latynina (USSR)—tie	18·732
1960	Latynina (USSR)	19·583
1964	Latynina (USSR)	19·599
1968	Caslavska (Czechoslovakia) and Petrik (USSR)	19·675

WEIGHTLIFTING

Bantamweight

		lbs
1948	de Pietro (USA)	678
1952	Udodov (USSR)	694½
1956	Vinci (USA)	754½
1960	Vinci (USA)	759
1964	Vachonin (USSR)	787¾
1968	Nassiri (Iran)	809¾

Featherweight

1920	de Haes (Belgium)	485
1924	Gabetti (Italy)*	887¼
1928	Andrysek (Austria)	633¾
1932	Suvigny (France)	633¾
1936	Terlazzo (USA)	689
1948	Fayad (Egypt)	733
1952	Chimischkian (USSR)	774
1956	Berger (USA)	776½
1960	Minajev (USSR)	819½
1964	Miyake (Japan)	876
1968	Miyake (Japan)	865

* total of 5 lifts

Lightweight

1920	Neyland (Estonia)	567¾
1924	Decottignies (France)*	970
1928	Helbig (Germany) and Haas (Austria)—tie	711
1932	Duverger (France)	716½
1936	Mesbah (Egypt) and Fein (Austria)—tie	755
1948	Shams (Egypt)	793½
1952	Kono (USA)	799
1956	Rybak (USSR)	837½
1960	Buschujev (USSR)	876
1964	Baszanowski (Poland)	953¼
1968	Baszanowski (Poland)	964¼

* total of 5 lifts

Middleweight

1920	Gance (France)	540
1924	Galimberti (Italy)*	1,085¾
1928	Roger (France)	738½
1932	Ismayr (Germany)	760½
1936	El Thouni (Egypt)	854¾
1948	Spellman (USA)	860
1952	George (USA)	882
1956	Bogdanovski (USSR)	925¾
1960	Kurynov (USSR)	964¼
1964	Zdrazila (Czechoslovakia)	980¾
1968	Kurenzov (USSR)	1,046¾

* total of 5 lifts

Light heavyweight

1920	Cadine (France)	639
1924	Rigoulot (France)*	1,107¾
1928	Nosseir (Egypt)	782½
1932	Hostin (France)	804¾
1936	Hostin (France)	820
1948	Stanczyk (USA)	920½
1952	Lomakin (USSR)	920½

1956	Kono (USA)	986¼
1960	Palinski (Poland)	975¼
1964	Plükfelder (USSR)	1,046
1968	Selitsky (USSR)	1,068¾
	* total of 5 lifts	

Middle heavyweight

1952	Schemansky (USA)	981
1956	Vorobjev (USSR)	1,019¼
1960	Vorobjev (USSR)	1,041¼
1964	Golovanov (USSR)	1,074
1968	Kangasniemi (Finland)	1,140½

Heavyweight

1920	Bottino (Italy)	595
1924	Tonani (Italy) *	1,140¾
1928	Strassberger (Germany)	810
1932	Skobla (Czechoslovakia)	837¾
1936	Manger (Germany)	903¾
1948	Davis (USA)	996½
1952	Davis (USA)	1,014
1956	Anderson (USA)	1,102
1960	Vlasov (USSR)	1,184½
1964	Zhabotinsky (USSR)	1,262
1968	Zhabotinsky (USSR)	1,261¾
	* total of 5 lifts	

SHOOTING

Free rifle

		Points
1896	Orphanidis (Greece)	1583
1900	Kellenberger (Switzerland)	930
1904	Event not held	
1908	Helgerud (Norway)	909
1912	Colas (France)	987
1920	Fisher (USA)	997
1924–1936	Event not held	
1948	Grünig (Switzerland)	1120
1952	Bogdanov (USSR)	1123
1956	Borisov (USSR)	1138
1960	Hammerer (Austria)	1129
1964	Anderson (USA)	1153
1968	Anderson (USA)	1157

Small-bore rifle (three positions)

1952	Kongshaug (Norway)	1164
1956	Bogdanov (USSR)	1172
1960	Schamburkin (USSR)	1149
1964	Wigger (USA)	1164
1968	Klinger (West Germany)	1157

Small-bore rifle (prone)

1912	Hird (USA)	194
1920	Nuesslein (USA)	391
1924	Coquelin de Lisle (France)	398
1928	Event not held	
1932	Rönnmark (Sweden)	294
1936	Rögeberg (Norway)	300
1948	Cook (USA)	599
1952	Sarbu (Rumania)	400
1956	Quelette (Canada)	600
1960	Kohnke (West Germany)	590
1964	Hammerl (Hungary)	597
1968	Kurka (Czechoslovakia)	598

Free pistol

1896	Paine (USA)	442
1900	Röderer (Switzerland)	503
1904–1908	Event not held	
1912	Lane (USA)	499
1920	Frederick (USA)	496
1924–1932	Event not held	
1936	Ullman (Sweden)	559
1948	Vasquez (Peru)	545
1952	Benner (USA)	553
1956	Linnosvuo (Finland)	556
1960	Gustchin (USSR)	560
1964	Markkanen (Finland)	560
1968	Kosich (USSR)	562

Rapid-fire pistol

1896	Phrangudis (Greece)	344
1900	Larouy (France)	58
1904	Event not held	
1908	van Asbrock (Belgium)	490
1912	Lane (USA)	499
1920	Paraense (Brazil)	274
1924	Bailey (USA)	18
1928	Event not held	
1932	Morigi (Italy)	42
1936	van Oyen (Germany)	36
1948	Takacs (Hungary)	580
1952	Takacs (Hungary)	579
1956	Petrescu (Rumania)	587
1960	McMillan (USA)	587
1964	Linnosvuo (Finland)	592
1968	Zapedski (Poland)	593

Clay pigeon

1900	Ewing (Canada)	
1904	Event not held	
1908	Ewing (Canada)	72
1912	Graham (USA)	96
1920	Arie (USA)	95
1924	Halasy (Hungary)	98
1928–1948	Event not held	
1952	Genereux (Canada)	192
1956	Rossini (Italy)	195
1960	Dumitrescu (Rumania)	192
1964	Mattarelli (Italy)	198
1968	Braithwaite (Great Britain)	198

Skeet

1968	Petrov (USSR)	198

FENCING

Team foil (women)

1960	USSR
1964	Hungary
1968	USSR

Individual foil (women)

		Wins
1924	Osiier (Denmark)	5
1928	Mayer (Germany)	7
1932	Preis (Austria)	9
1936	Schacherer-Elek (Hungary)	6
1948	Elek (Hungary)	6
1952	Camber (Italy)	5
1956	Sheen (Great Britain)	6
1960	Schmid (West Germany)	6
1964	Ujlaki-Rejtö (Hungary)	4
1968	Novikova (USSR)	4

Team foil (men)

1904	Cuba
1908—1912	Event not held
1920	Italy
1924	France
1928	Italy
1932	France
1936	Italy
1948	France
1952	France
1956	Italy
1960	USSR
1964	USSR
1968	France

Individual foil (men)

1896	Gravelotte (France)	4
1900	Coste (France)	6
1904	Fonst (Cuba)	2
1908	Event not held	
1912	Nadi (Italy)	7
1920	Nadi (Italy)	10
1924	Ducret (France)	6
1928	Gaudin (France)	9
1932	Marzi (Italy)	9
1936	Gaudini (Italy)	7
1948	Buhan (France)	7
1952	d'Oriola (France)	8
1956	d'Oriola (France)	6
1960	Zdanovitsch (USSR)	6
1964	Franke (Poland)	3
1968	Drimba (Rumania)	4

Team épée

1908	France
1912	Belgium
1920	Italy
1924	France
1928	Italy
1932	France
1936	Italy
1948	France

1952	Italy	
1956	Italy	
1960	Italy	
1964	Hungary	
1968	Hungary	

Individual épée

1900	Fonst (Cuba)	
1904	Fonst (Cuba)	
1908	Alibert (France)	5
1912	Anspach (Belgium)	6
1920	Massard (France)	
1924	Delporte (Belgium)	
1928	Gaudin (France)	8
1932	Cornaggia-Medici (Italy)	9
1936	Riccardi (Italy)	13
1948	Cantone (Italy)	7
1952	Mangiarotti (Italy)	7
1956	Pavesi (Italy)	5
1960	Delfino (Italy)	5
1964	Kriss (USSR)	5
1968	Kulcsar (Hungary)	4

Team sabre

1908	Hungary
1912	Hungary
1920	Italy
1924	Italy
1928	Hungary
1932	Hungary
1936	Hungary
1948	Hungary
1952	Hungary
1956	Hungary
1960	Hungary
1964	USSR
1968	USSR

Individual sabre

1896	Georgiadis (Greece)	4
1900	de la Falaise (France)	
1904	Diaz (Cuba)	
1908	Fuchs (Hungary)	6
1912	Fuchs (Hungary)	6
1920	Nadi (Italy)	11
1924	Posta (Hungary)	5
1928	Tersztyansky (Hungary)	9
1932	Piller (Hungary)	8
1936	Kabos (Hungary)	7
1948	Gerevich (Hungary)	7
1952	Kovacs (Hungary)	8
1956	Karpati (Hungary)	6
1960	Karpati (Hungary)	5
1964	Pezsa (Hungary)	2
1968	Pawlowski (Poland)	4

MODERN PENTATHLON

Individual

1912	Lilliehöök (Sweden)	27
1920	Dryssen (Sweden)	18
1924	Lindman (Sweden)	18
1928	Thofelt (Sweden)	47
1932	Oxenstierna (Sweden)	32
1936	Handrick (Germany)	31·5
1948	Grut (Sweden)	16
1952	Hall (Sweden)	32
1956	Hall (Sweden)	4833
1960	Nemeth (Hungary)	5024
1964	Török (Hungary)	5116
1968	Ferm (Sweden)	4964

Team

1952	Hungary	166
1956	USSR	13,645·5
1960	Hungary	14,863
1964	USSR	14,961
1968	Hungary	14,325

RIDING

Three-day event (individual)

1912	Nordlander (Sweden)	46·59
1920	Mörner (Sweden)	1775·00
1924	van Zijp (Netherlands)	1976·00
1928	de Mortanges (Netherlands)	1969·82
1932	de Mortanges (Netherlands)	1813·83
1936	Stubbendorf (Germany)	362·30
1948	Chevallier (France)	4
1952	von Blixen-Finecke (Sweden)	28·33
1956	Kastenman (Sweden)	66·53
1960	Morgan (Australia)	7·15
1964	Checcoli (Italy)	64·40
1968	Guyon (France)	38·86

Three-day event (team)

1912	Sweden	139·06
1920	Sweden	5057·00
1924	Netherlands	5297·50
1928	Netherlands	5865·68
1932	USA	5038·08
1936	Germany	676·65
1948	USA	161·50
1952	Sweden	221·94
1956	Great Britain	355·48
1960	Australia	128·18
1964	Italy	85·80
1968	Great Britain	175·93

Dressage – individual

1912	Bonde (Sweden)	15·00
1920	Lundblad (Sweden)	27,937·00
1924	von Linder (Sweden)	276·4
1928	von Langen (Germany)	237·42
1932	Lesage (France)	343·75
1936	Pollay (Germany)	352·00
1948	Moser (Switzerland)	492·5
1952	St Cyr (Sweden)	561·0
1956	St Cyr (Sweden)	860·0
1960	Filatov (USSR)	2144
1964	Chammartin (Switzerland)	1504
1968	Kisimov (USSR)	1572

Dressage – team

1928	Germany	669·72
1932	France	2818·75
1936	Germany	5074
1948	France	1269
1952	Sweden	1597·5
1956	Sweden	2475
1960	Event not held	
1964	West Germany	2558
1968	West Germany	2699

Grand Prix jumping – individual

1912	Cariou (France)
1920	Lequio (Italy)
1924	Gemuseus (Switzerland)
1928	Ventura (Czechoslovakia)
1932	Nishi (Japan)
1936	Hasse (Germany)
1948	Mariles-Cortes (Mexico)
1952	d'Oriola (France)
1956	Winkler (West Germany)
1960	R. d'Inzeo (Italy)
1964	d'Oriola (France)
1968	Steinkraus (USA)

Grand Prix jumping – team

1912	Sweden
1920	Sweden
1924	Sweden
1928	Spain
1932	All teams disqualified
1936	Germany
1948	Mexico
1952	Great Britain
1956	West Germany
1960	West Germany
1964	West Germany
1968	Canada

TEAM SPORTS

Water polo

1900	Great Britain
1904	USA
1908	Great Britain
1912	Great Britain
1920	Great Britain
1924	France
1928	Germany
1932	Hungary
1936	Hungary
1948	Italy
1952	Hungary
1956	Hungary
1960	Italy
1964	Hungary
1968	Yugoslavia

Hockey

1908	Great Britain
1912	Event not held
1920	Great Britain
1924	Event not held
1928	India
1932	India

1936	India
1948	India
1952	India
1956	India
1960	Pakistan
1964	India
1968	Pakistan

Volleyball (Women)

1964	Japan
1968	USSR

Volleyball (Men)

1964	USSR
1968	USSR

Basketball

1904–1968 USA

Football

1900	Great Britain
1904	Canada
1908	Great Britain
1912	Great Britain
1920	Belgium
1924	Uruguay
1928	Uruguay
1932	Event not held
1936	Italy
1948	Sweden
1952	Hungary
1956	USSR
1960	Yugoslavia
1964	Hungary
1968	Hungary

THE WINTER OLYMPIC GAMES

I.	Chamonix	1924
II.	St Moritz	1928
III.	Lake Placid	1932
IV.	Garmisch-Partenkirchen	1936
V.	St Moritz	1948
VI.	Oslo	1952
VII.	Cortina d'Ampezzo	1956
VIII.	Squaw Valley	1960
IX.	Innsbruck	1964
X.	Grenoble	1968

ALPINE SKIING (MEN)

Downhill

1948	Oreiller (France)
1952	Colo (Italy)
1956	Sailer (Austria)
1960	Vuarnet (France)
1964	Zimmermann (Austria)
1968	Killy (France)

Giant slalom

1952	Eriksen (Norway)
1956	Sailer (Austria)
1960	Staub (Switzerland)
1964	Bonlieu (France)
1968	Killy (France)

Slalom

1948	Reinalter (Switzerland)
1952	Schneider (Austria)
1956	Sailer (Austria)
1960	Hinterseer (Austria)
1964	Stiegler (Austria)
1968	Killy (France)

ALPINE SKIING (WOMEN)

Downhill

1948	Schlunegger (Switzerland)
1952	Jochum-Beiser (Austria)
1956	Berthod (Switzerland)
1960	Biebl (West Germany)
1964	Haas (Austria)
1968	Pall (Austria)

Giant slalom

1952	Lawrence—Mead (USA)
1956	Reichert (West Germany)
1960	Rüegg (Switzerland)
1964	M. Goitschel (France)
1968	Greene (Canada)

Slalom

1948	Frazer (USA)
1952	Lawrence—Mead (USA)
1956	Colliard (Switzerland)
1960	Heggveit (Canada)
1964	Chr. Goitschel (France)
1968	M. Goitschel (France)

NORDIC SKIING (MEN)

15 km cross-country

		Minutes
1956	Brenden (Norway)	49:39·0
1960	Brusveen (Norway)	51:55·5
1964	Mäntyranta (Finland)	50:54·1
1968	Grönningen (Norway)	47:54·2

18 km cross-country

		Hours
1924	Haug (Norway)	1:14:31
1928	Gröttumsbraaten (Norway)	1:37:01
1932	Utterström (Sweden)	1:23:07
1936	Larsson (Sweden)	1:14:38
1948	Lundström (Sweden)	1:13:50
1952	Brenden (Norway)	1:01:34

30 km cross-country

1956	Hakulinen (Finland)	1:44:06
1960	Jernberg (Sweden)	1:51:03·9
1964	Mäntyranta (Finland)	1:30:50·7
1968	Nones (Italy)	1:35:39·2

50 km cross-country

1924	Haug (Norway)	3:44:32
1928	Hedlund (Sweden)	4:52:03
1932	Saarinen (Finland)	4:28:00
1936	Viklund (Sweden)	3:30:11
1948	Karlsson (Sweden)	3:47:47
1952	Hakulinen (Finland)	3:33:33
1956	Jernberg (Sweden)	2:50:27
1960	Hämäläinen (Finland)	2:59:06·3
1964	Jernberg (Sweden)	2:43:52·6
1968	Ellefsäter (Norway)	2:28:45·8

4 × 10 (40) km Relay

1936	Finland	2:41:33
1948	Sweden	2:32:08
1952	Finland	2:20:16
1956	USSR	2:15:30
1960	Finland	2:18:45·6
1964	Sweden	2:18:34·6
1968	Norway	2:08:33·5

Nordic Combined (cross-country and jumping)

		Points
1924	Haug (Norway)	453·8
1928	Gröttumsbraaten (Norway)	427·8
1932	Gröttumsbraaten (Norway)	446·2
1936	Hagen (Norway)	430·3
1948	Hasu (Finland)	448·8
1952	Slättvik (Norway)	451·621
1956	Stenersen (Norway)	455·000
1960	Thoma (West Germany)	457·952
1964	Knutsen (Norway)	469·28
1968	Keller (West Germany)	449·04

Ski jumping (small hill)

1924	Thams (Norway)	49 +49 m	227·5
1928	Andersen (Norway)	60 +64 m	230·5
1932	B. Rouud (Norway)	66·5+69 m	228·0
1936	B. Rouud (Norway)	75 +74·5 m	232·0
1948	Hugsted (Norway)	65 +70 m	228·1
1952	Bergmann (Norway)	67·5+68 m	226·0
1956	Hyvärinen (Finland)	81 +84 m	227·0
1960	Recknagel (W. Germany)	93·5+84·5 m	227·2
1964	Kankkonen (Finland)	80 +79 m	229·9
1968	Raska (Czechoslovakia)	79 +72·5 m	216·5

Ski jumping (big hill)

1964	Engan (Norway)	93·5+90·5 m	230·7
1968	Beloussov (USSR)	101·5+98·5 m	231·3

Biathlon

		Hours
1960	Lestander (Sweden)	1:33:21·6
1964	Melanin (USSR)	1:20:26·8
1968	Solberg (Norway)	1:13:45·9

Biathlon-Relay

1968	USSR	2:13:02·4

NORDIC SKIING (WOMEN)

5 km cross-country

		Minutes
1964	Bojarskich (USSR)	17:50·5
1968	Gustafsson (Sweden)	16:45·2

10 km cross-country

1952	Wideman (Finland)	41:40·0
1956	Kosyrjeva (USSR)	38:11·0
1960	Gusakova (USSR)	39:46·6
1964	Bojarskich (USSR)	40:24·3

1968	Gustafsson (Sweden)	36:46·5

3×5 (15) km Relay

1956	Finland	1:09:01·0
1960	Sweden	1:04:21·4
1964	USSR	59:20·2
1968	Norway	57:30·0

SPEED SKATING (MEN)

500 m

1924	Jewtraw (USA)	44·0
1928	Thunberg (Finland) and Evensen (Norway)—tie	43·4
1932	Shea (USA)	43·4
1936	Ballangrud (Norway)	43·4
1948	Helgesen (Norway)	43·1
1952	Henry (USA)	43·2
1956	Grischin (USSR)	40·2
1960	Grischin (USSR)	40·2
1964	McDermott (USA)	40·1
1968	Keller (West Germany)	40·3

1500 m

1924	Thunberg (Finland)	2:20·8
1928	Thunberg (Finland)	2:21·1
1932	Shea (USA)	2:57·5
1936	Mathisen (Norway)	2:19·2
1948	Farstad (Norway)	2:17·6
1952	Andersen (Norway)	2:20·4
1956	Grischin and Mikhailov (USSR)	2:08·6
1960	Grischin (USSR) and Aas (Norway)	2:10·4
1964	Antson (USSR)	2:10·3
1968	Verkerk (Netherlands)	2:03·4

5000 m

1924	Thunberg (Finland)	8:39·0
1928	Ballangrud (Norway)	8:50·5
1932	Jaffee (USA)	9:40·8
1936	Ballangrud (Norway)	8:19·6
1948	Liaklev (Norway)	8:29·4
1952	Andersen (Norway)	8:10·6
1956	Schilkov (USSR)	7:48·7
1960	Kositschkin (USSR)	7:51·3
1964	Johannesen (Norway)	7:38·4
1968	Maier (Norway)	7:22·4

10,000 m

1924	Skutnabb (Finland)	18:04·8
1928	Event not held	
1932	Jaffee (USA)	19:13·6
1936	Ballangrud (Norway)	17:24·3
1948	Seyffarth (Sweden)	17:26·3
1952	Andersen (Norway)	16:45·8
1956	Ericsson (Sweden)	16:35·9
1960	Johannesen (Norway)	15:46·4
1964	Nilsson (Sweden)	15:50·1
1968	Höglin (Sweden)	15:23·6

SPEED SKATING (WOMEN)

500 m		Seconds
1960	Haase (West Germany)	45·9
1964	Skoblikova (USSR)	45·0
1968	Titova (USSR)	46·1

1000 m		Minutes
1960	Guseva (USSR)	1:34·1
1964	Skoblikova (USSR)	1:33·2
1968	Geijssen (Netherlands)	1:32·6

1500 m

1960	Skoblikova (USSR)	2:25·2
1964	Skoblikova (USSR)	2:22·6
1968	Mustonen (Finland)	2:22·4

3000 m

1960	Skoblikova (USSR)	5:13·9
1964	Skoblikova (USSR)	5:14·9
1968	Schut (Netherlands)	4:56·2

FIGURE SKATING

Men		Points
1908	Salchow (Sweden)	2641·00
1920	Grafström (Sweden)	2838·50
1924	Grafström (Sweden)	2575·25
1928	Grafström (Sweden)	2698·25
1932	Schäfer (Austria)	2602·00
1936	Schäfer (Austria)	2659·00
1948	Button (USA)	191·177
1952	Button (USA)	192·256
1956	A. Jenkins (USA)	166·43
1960	D. Jenkins (USA)	1440·2
1964	Schnelldorfer (West Germany)	1916·9
1968	Schwarz (Austria)	1904·1

Women

1908	Syers (Great Britain)	1767·50
1920	Julin (Sweden)	1278·90
1924	Planck-Szabo (Austria)	2094·25
1928	Henie (Norway)	2452·25
1932	Henie (Norway)	2302·50
1936	Henie (Norway)	2971·4
1948	Scott (Canada)	163·077
1952	Altwegg (Great Britain)	161·756
1956	Albright (USA)	169·97
1960	Heiss (USA)	1490·1
1964	Dijkstra (Netherlands)	2018·5
1968	Fleming (USA)	1970·5

Pairs

1908	Hübler/Burger (Germany)	78·4
1920	Jacobson/Jacobson (Finland)	80·7
1924	Engelmann/Berger (Austria)	74·5
1928	Joly/Brunet (France)	78·2
1932	Brunet/Brunet (France)	76·7
1936	Herber/Baier (Germany)	103·3
1948	Lannoy/Baugniet (Belgium)	11·227
1952	Falk/Falk (West Germany)	11·400
1956	Schwarz/Oppelt (Austria)	11·31
1960	Wagner/Paul (Canada)	80·4
1964	Belousova/Protopopov (USSR)	104·4
1968	Belousova/Protopopov (USSR)	315·2

ICE HOCKEY

1920	Canada
1924	Canada
1928	Canada
1932	Canada
1936	Great Britain
1948	Canada
1952	Canada
1956	USSR
1960	USA
1964	USSR
1968	USSR

BOBSLED

Two-man		Minutes
1932	USA I (J. Stevens/C. Stevens)	8:14·74
1936	USA I (Brown/Washbond)	5:29·29
1948	Switzerland II (Endrich/Waller)	5:29·2
1952	Germany I (Ostler/Nieberl)	5:24·54
1956	Italy I (Dalla Costa/Conti)	5:30·14
1960	Event not held	
1964	Great Britain I (Nash/Dixon)	4:21·90
1968	Italy I (Monti/de Paolis)	4:41·54

Four-man

1924	Switzerland I	5:45·54
1928	USA II	3:20·5
1932	USA I	7:53·68
1936	Switzerland II	5:19·85
1948	USA II	5:20·1
1952	West Germany I	5:07·84
1956	Switzerland I	5:10·44
1960	Event not held	
1964	Canada I	4:14·46
1968	Italy I	2:17·39

TOBOGGANING

Single-seater (men)

1964	Köhler (West Germany)	3:26·77
1968	Schmid (Austria)	2:52·48

Two-seater (men)

1964	Austria (Feistmantl/Stengl)	1:41·62
1968	East Germany (Bonsack/Köhler)	1:35·85

Single-seater (women)

1964	Enderlein (West Germany)	3:24·67
1968	Lechner (Italy)	2:28·66

ACKNOWLEDGEMENTS

Erich Baumann, Ludvigsburg: cover picture and endpapers, pp. 2, 6, 8 (bottom), 22 and 23 (all five photos), 24, 51, 56 (top), 62 (left), 64, 85 (bottom), 89, 90, 94 (top), 96 (both photos), 97, 100. Anthony-Verlag, Starnberg: p. 10 (bottom). Camera Press: pp. 38, 46, 50 (top). Franz Fink, Vienna: p. 102. Ghedina, Cortina D'Ampezzo: p. 43. Wolfgang Girardi, Innsbruck: pp. 35, 51 (top), 57 (top). Keystone, Munich: pp. 8 (top), 15 (left and right), 28, 48, 72 (top left), 73 (bottom), 106 (bottom), 110 (bottom). E. D. Lacey, Bookham: p. 81. Friederike Lukan, Vienna: pp. 16 (bottom), 17 (top and bottom). Max Mühlberger, Munich: pp. 61, 93, 108. Oesterreichischer Bundesverlag, Archiv, Vienna: pp. 9 (top), 33, 37 (bottom left), 56 (left), 63, 84 (top). 20th Olympics Committee, Munich: pp. 77, 79 (bottom), 80, 112. 11th Winter Olympics Committee, Sapporo: pp. 70 (top and bottom), 71 (top and bottom), 112. Fritz Prenzel, Munich: p. 74. Fred Rieder, Salzburg: p. 106 (top left). Alois Rottensteiner, Vienna: pp. 26 (top and bottom), 29, 31 (left), 55, 58 (top and bottom), 59 (top), 67 (top and bottom), 69 (top), 76 (centre and bottom), 79 (top), 84 (bottom), 85 (top), 87, 88 (top right), 104 (top), 107, 111 (top and bottom). A. F. Rottensteiner, Vienna: p. 99 (both photos). Lothar Rubelt, Vienna: pp. 11, 12, 31 (right), 37 (bottom right), 41, 44 (all three photos), 45 (top), 47, 50 (bottom), 51 (bottom), 67 (centre), 68 (top and bottom), 72 (top right), 73 (top), 76 (top), 105 (top), 110 (top). Schirner, Berlin: pp. 27, 30 (left), 32, 34 (top and bottom), 37 (top), 40 (all four photos), 60, 94 (bottom). Staatsbibliotek, Berlin: pp. 10 (top), 14 (bottom), 16 (top left and right), 20 (top), 21 (top and bottom). Through the courtesy of the International Olympics Committee: p. 82. Ullstein-Archiv, Berlin: p. 18. UPI, Frankfurt/M: pp. 53, 88 (top left and centre). Votava, Vienna: pp. 9 (bottom), 20 (centre and bottom), 30 (right), 36, 42, 45 (bottom), 49, 52, 57 (bottom), 59 (bottom), 62 (right), 69 (bottom), 72 (bottom), 86 (top and bottom), 88 (bottom), 92, 98, 103, 104 (bottom), 105 (bottom, both photos), 100 (top right). Graphics: Wolfgang Bucek, Vienna.
1972 Section Keystone Press: pp. 6, 8, 14. Stern magazine: p. 9. Syndication International: pp. 12, 15. UPI, London: pp. 4–5, 7, 10, 11 (bottom), 16 (top). Votava, Vienna: 1, 2, 3, 4 (top), 8 (bottom), 11 (top), 16 (bottom).

INDEX